PROVENCE

TWELVE JOURNEYS WITH A GASTRONOME

To Antoinette

MICHAEL RAFFAEL

PROVENCE

TWELVE JOURNEYS WITH A GASTRONOME

Published in 1990 by
George Philip Limited
59 Grosvenor Street,
London W1X 9DA

British Library Cataloguing in Publication Data

Raffael, Michael
Provence: twelve journeys with a gastronome.
1. France. Provence. Description & travel
I. Title
914.4′904838

ISBN 0-540-01187-8

Cover: Marianne Majerus' photograph hand tinted by W. J. Payne.
Maps by John Gilkes, based on George Philip cartography.
Illustrations by Shirley Barker.
Designed by Vivienne Brar.

Printed and bound in Great Britain
by Butler & Tanner Ltd, Frome and London

ACKNOWLEDGEMENTS

Thanks to: Simone Lemaire, Robin Yapp, the Monteillet family, M. and Mme Paul Joyet, Priscilla Eissen, Jane Eakin, Jean-Yves Cannepin, Odile Bordes, Elisabeth Bourgeois, René Jouveau, Yves Guieu, Henri Pawlowski, M. and Mme Georges Delille, M. and Mme Claude Campanile, and the Fondation Escoffier. Thanks also to Andrew Sutterby, John Gaisford and Jude Welton at George Philip.

CONTENTS

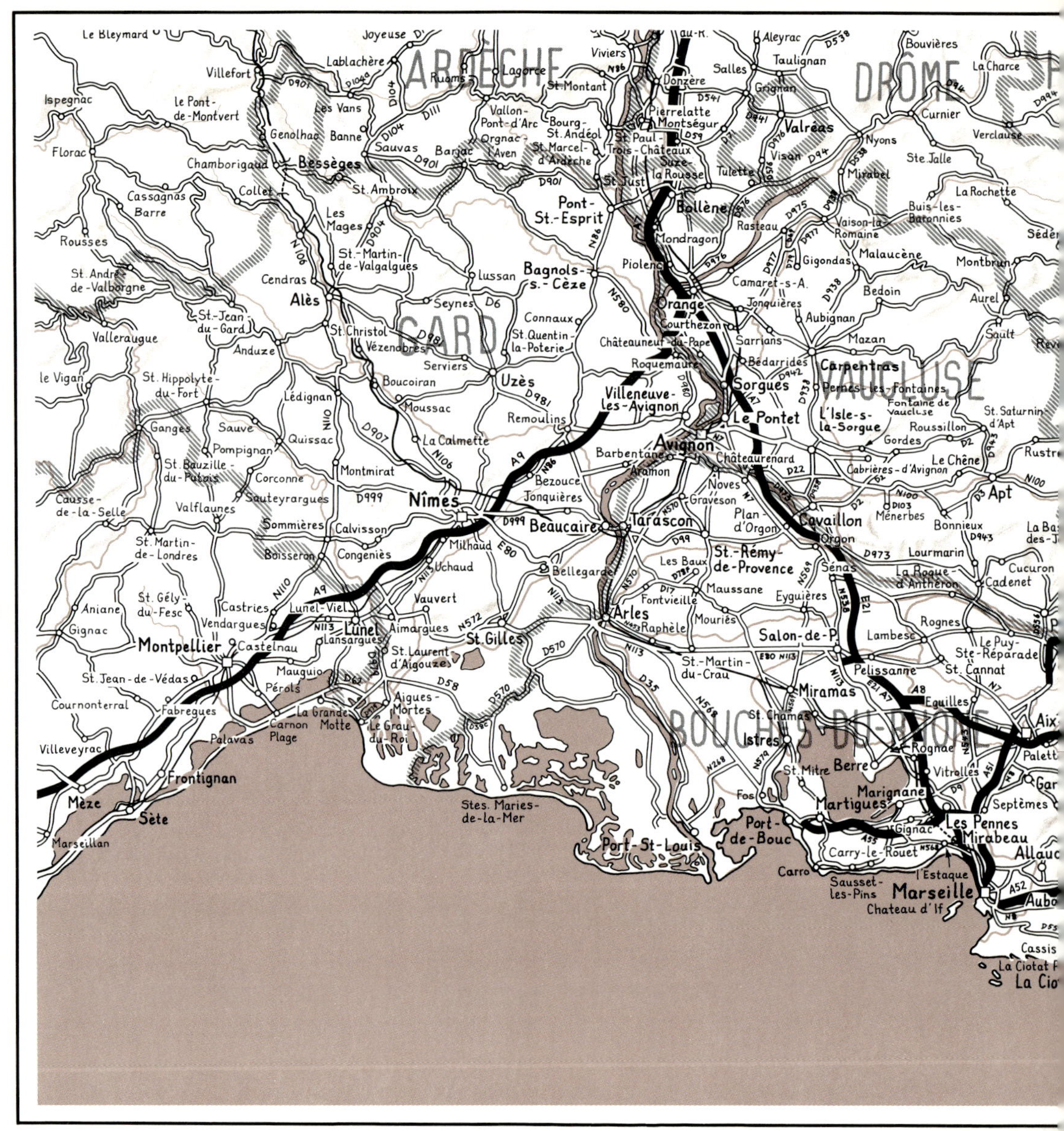

ARDÈCHE
DRÔME
GARD
VAUCLUSE
BOUCHES-DU-RHÔNE
Le Bleymard
Joyeuse
Aleyrac
Bouvières
La Charce
Villefort
Lablachère
Ruoms
Lagorce
Viviers
Donzère
Salles
Taulignan
Ispegnac
le Pont-de-Montvert
Les Vans
St. Montant
Pierrelatte
Montségur
Grignan
Curnier
Verclause
Florac
Genolhac
Banne
Vallon-Pont-d'Arc
Orgnac-l'Aven
Bourg-St. Andéol
St. Marcel-d'Ardèche
St. Paul-Trois-Châteaux
Valréas
Visan
Nyons
Chamborigaud
Bessèges
Sauvas
Barjac
Suze-la Rousse
Tulette
Ste. Jalle
Mirabel
Cassagnas
Barre
Collet
St. Ambroix
St. Just
Pont-St.-Esprit
Bollène
Rasteau
Vaison-la-Romaine
Buis-les-Baronnies
La Rochette
Rousses
Les Mages
Mondragon
Gigondas
Malaucène
Montbrun
St. André-de-Valborgne
St.-Martin-de-Valgalgues
Lussan
Bagnols-s.-Cèze
Piolenc
Camaret-s-A.
Cendras
Alès
Seynes
Orange
Jonquières
Bedoin
Aurel
St.-Jean-du-Gard
Valleraugue
St. Christol
Vézenobres
Connaux
St. Quentin-la-Poterie
Courthezon
Aubignan
Châteauneuf-du-Pape
Sarrians
Mazan
Sault
Anduze
Serviers
Roquemaure
Bédarrides
Carpentras
le Vigan
St. Hippolyte-du-Fort
Boucoiran
Uzès
Villeneuve-les-Avignon
Sorgues
Pernes-les-Fontaines
Fontaine de Vaucluse
Lédignan
Moussac
Remoulins
Le Pontet
L'Isle-s-la-Sorgue
Roussillon
St. Saturnin-d'Apt
Ganges
Sauve
Quissac
La Calmette
Avignon
Gordes
Pompignan
Barbentane
Aramon
Châteaurenard
Cabrières-d'Avignon
Le Chêne
St. Bauzille-du-Putois
Corconne
Montmirat
Bezouce
Noves
Apt
Causse-de-la-Selle
Sauteyrargues
Nîmes
Jonquières
Graveson
Valflaunes
Sommières
Calvisson
Beaucaire
Tarascon
Plan-d'Orgon
Cavaillon
Ménerbes
Bonnieux
St. Martin-de-Londres
Milhaud
Orgon
St.-Rémy-de-Provence
Boisseron
Congeniès
Uchaud
Bellegarde
Les Baux
Sénas
Lourmarin
La Roque-d'Anthéron
Cucuron
Cadenet
St. Gély-du-Fesc
Castries
Lunel-Viel
Vauvert
Maussane
Fontvieille
Eyguières
Aniane
Gignac
Vendargues
Lunel
Aimargues
Arles
Raphèle
Mouriès
Rognes
Lambesc
Salon-de-P.
Montpellier
Castelnau
Lansargues
St. Gilles
St. Laurent-d'Aigouze
St.-Martin-du-Crau
Le Puy-Ste-Réparade
St. Jean-de-Védas
Mauguio
Pérols
Pelissanne
St. Cannat
Cournonterral
Fabregues
Aigues-Mortes
Miramas
Eguilles
Carnon Plage
La Grande Motte
Le Grau-du-Roi
St. Chamas
Aix
Palavas
Istres
Rognac
Villeveyrac
Berre
Vitrolles
St. Mitre
Frontignan
Marignane
Septèmes
Mèze
Fos
Martigues
Les Pennes Mirabeau
Sète
Stes. Maries-de-la-Mer
Port-de-Bouc
Gignac
Marseillan
Port-St-Louis
Carry-le-Rouet
Carro
Sausset-les-Pins
l'Estaque
Marseille
Chateau d'If
Cassis
La Ciotat

PROVENCE

Provence was the first Province (hence the name) that the Romans established outside their homeland. It is flanked by Languedoc and Italy, but the exact definition of Provence's boundaries is still a matter of dispute. Everyone agrees that the Rhône marks its western limit, but how far east does it extend? For some, Provence stops at the River Var. Like many others, I've chosen to include the Côte d'Azur and the mountain villages on the border, where the Italian culinary connection still thrives alongside Provençal tradition.

STARTING OUT

French regional cookery was 'invented' by Edmond Sailland, better known as Curnonsky. This Prince of Gastronomes, a boulevardier with the girth of a rhino, and the palate – metaphorically speaking – of a ballerina, scoured the provinces between the wars, identifying the *goûts de terroir*, the distinctive, 'flavours of the soil'. His 28-volume *La France Gastronomique* not only gave identity to provincial food as opposed to Haute Cuisine, it also endorsed regional specialities. It was a worthy cause, but one with some ironic consequences. Restaurants began to feature 'regional specialities', and when these did not exist, they invented them. Endorsements from Curnonsky could transform a local delicacy into an international industry. The Provençal town of Montélimar, for example, is renowned for its nougat. Yet the standardized, international version rarely equals that made by local confiseurs who use honey (especially acacia) rather than sugar, and heat it gently so its aroma survives.

The culinary landscape Curnonsky painted of Provence was, even then, in part an artificial, bourgeois vision at least one step removed from the rural original. The *aïoli* enjoyed by the first generation of middle-class Parisians to spend their holidays in the Midi was *le grand aïoli*; garlic mayonnaise served with salt cod, snails, artichokes, and sometimes a leg of lamb. The simple rustic version – a garlic sauce with potatoes, carrots and whatever other vegetables might be at hand – wouldn't have appealed.

And it wouldn't have appealed to me to embark upon a gastronomic tour by following Curnonsky's footsteps. My appetite is less dependent upon scenting a roast partridge or catching sight of a plate of raviolis stuffed with wild mushrooms than on a two-hour walk and no breakfast. The artful feasts of 'Provençal cuisine' presented at many of the exquisite, expensive restaurants have their place, but, except on special occasions, I prefer less sophisticated delights; food that's firmly rooted in the traditions and raw materials of the region.

There *are* traditional, distinct flavours to Provençal cooking, whether it's served in a three-star restaurant or in a station buffet. The taste of olive-oil permeates every salad. Garlic, in the soup or on the waiter's breath, is omnipresent. Fleshy marmande tomatoes from the plains between Carpentras and Cavaillon are constant features. Wild herbs plucked from the *garrigues* flavour every *daube*, every *ragoût*, every plump fish hissing on the grill.

Some of the basic ingredients are disappearing. There are less than half the number of olive trees that there were 30 years ago, for example. And natural stocks of game are being depleted by the French passion for hunting. Thrushes – a popular, though illegal culinary treat in Provence – have shrunk from being the sixth most common species of British birds to the thirteenth, simply because they winter in the South of France. On my first visit to Cannes as a boy, my parents bought sea urchins, and we sat on a beach scooping the soft, orange stars from the spiny shells with a spoon. They were an accessible delicacy then, but now they're becoming scarce along the Côte d'Azur.

Change isn't always for the worse, though. There was a time in the 1960s, for instance, when as one forthright commentator put it, 'there was a corrupt, mercenary mafia which started pissing waves of cheap rosé, shamelessly called "*rosé de Provence*"'. Rosés, now produced by a new generation of technically expert wine growers, have returned to critical favour. These skilled and dedicated wine-makers are not afraid to experiment with red and white wines too. Their vintages are already challenging the reputed wines of Provence – the Châteauneuf du Pape, Vacqueryas, Bandols, Cassis, and the like. And even within these traditional regions, new trends and tastes emerge – towards white Châteauneuf du Pape, for example, or organic wines in Bandol. Finding a good vineyard, as yet 'undiscovered', can bring almost as much self-satisfaction to the finder as the growers feel when they first taste the fruits of a successful vintage.

The same can be said of discovering the taste of Provence off the beaten track. I've always travelled like a discriminating hippie, planning a route, but never afraid to leave it if something interesting turns up. The measure of uncertainty mitigates the occasional disappointments and certainly heightens the pleasure. It would be coy of me to pretend that I moved around Provence as a gastronomical virgin, but I have tried to retain a sense of freshness by seeking out unfamiliar faces, places and tastes. The addresses and wine lists in the margins will help you find them too.

1

TRUFFLES IN TRICASTIN

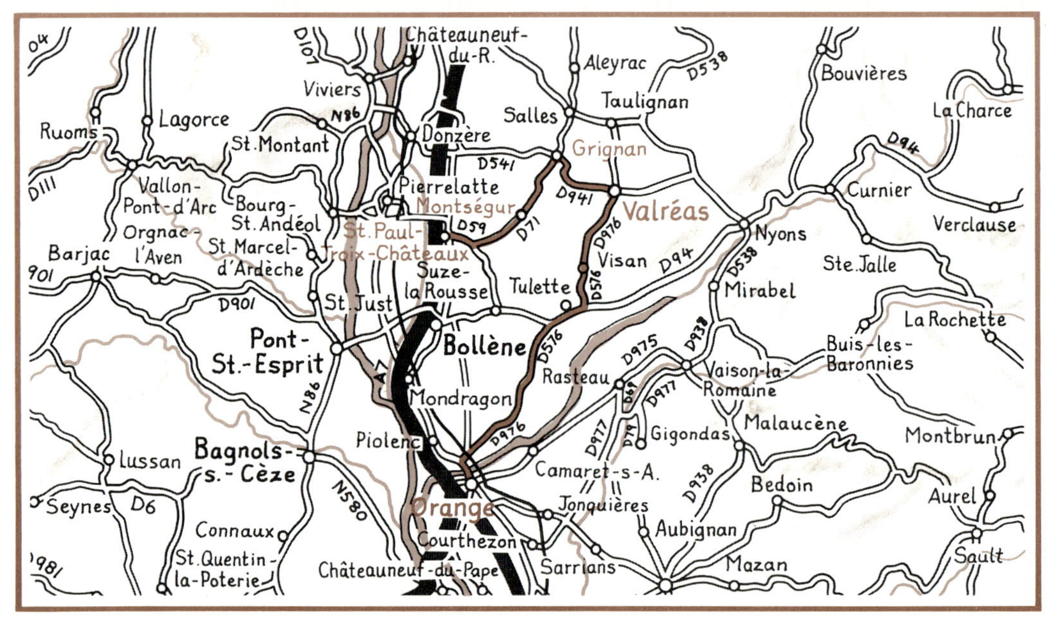

Orange – Valréas – Grignan – St Paul-Troix-Châteaux – Montségur – Grignan

Looking at modern Orange, prosperous capital of the Côtes du Rhône wine growing region, manicured for the tourists who pass through this 'Gateway to Provence', it's hard to identify it with the poverty, plague and religious persecutions which characterized its history. But to begin to grasp the wealth and vitality of Provençal food as experienced by today's inhabitants, it helps to sympathize with the hunger from which it emerged.

'I never', wrote the Regency traveller, John Hughes, after visiting Orange, 'beheld a more squalid, uncivilized, ferocious looking people. A grin or a cannibal scowl, seems almost universally to disfigure features, which are none of the best or cleanest.' The patronne of the *Croix Blanche* there was 'as mean and dirty as the hole in which she lived.'

Nor should Hughes have been too surprised by what he encountered. During the French Revolution, only a few years before his visit, the citizens had penned 332 nuns, priests and other assorted prisoners in the Roman theatre which stands in the centre of the town, before guillotining them in the main square.

Times have changed, but echoes of Orange's past remain. Near the Roman theatre, in the centre of the town, is a smart little restaurant, *L'Aigo-Boulido*. In Provençal, the patois which sounds like a patchwork of all the Latin languages stitched into its own loose-fitting Esperanto, the words mean 'boiled water'. According to a local saying of the apple-a-day variety, 'Boiled water saves life'. Flavoured with garlic, sage and an arabesque of olive-oil, it was a thin broth swallowed with a crust of bread as a last resort when the larder was otherwise empty. Perhaps either as a reminder of what was in store for them, or so that they could grow acquainted with each other's breath right from the start, *aigo-boulido* was traditionally served to newly weds.

L'Aigo-Boulido
20 PLACE SILVAIN
84100 ORANGE
TELEPHONE 90 34 10 34

There exists a bourgeois version of the soup, enriched with eggs: the garlic gives the liquid a sweet, rather than assertive flavour; eggs and oil combine to create a light, silky touch, and the herbs provide the personality. But it did not figure on the restaurant menu. The owner's wife lamented that her regular customers, those who kept the restaurant afloat once the tourists had finished their summer migration, did not want to dine on 'the old dishes'. They wanted a *demi-lune* of Breton scallops, langoustines from Scotland, *foie gras* from Périgord and pink peppercorns. And why not? The same proverb which recommends the restorative qualities of *aigo-boulido* warns that too much of a good thing can be dangerous: 'After a while it kills people.'

Commonplace dishes of yesteryear, such as *aigo-boulido*, are more likely to disappear than those which were reserved for celebrations. *Oreillettes*, 'little ears', dangle somewhere between traditional Provençal food and its updated facsimile. Parchment-crisp, stippled with blisters, powdered with icing sugar, and tasting of orange flower water, these pastry ribbons were once a special treat at baptisms and over the New Year, when they were piled in a basket under a white cloth. Now they are sold routinely by patisseries in the *département* of Vaucluse.

J. Duffe
RUE PONT NEUF
84100 ORANGE

On the corner of the Rue Pont Neuf, is a small patisserie, *J. Duffe*, which offers the crispest *oreillettes* in Orange. Madame behind the counter explained that they had been pinned out by hand. 'They take a long time to prepare,' she said, 'which is why we do them less often.' Since the dough needs rolling until it is almost strudel-fine, before being cut into strips and fried, it is easy to understand the shopkeeper's reservations. Apart from their brittle, wafer-thin texture, these are probably the neatest *oreillettes* I've ever tried; they curl elegantly, and their surface has a landscape of tiny air-pockets spread over it rather than the swollen bubbles which lesser bakers sometimes achieve.

Le Bec Fin
14 RUE SEGOND-WEBER
84100 ORANGE
TELEPHONE 90 34 14 76

I encountered another facet of Provence's evolving culinary heritage in a back-street bistro. *Le Bec Fin* is not the kind of place which attracts the praises of the guides, but Auresians like it, and even voted it their favourite eating house one year. Its menu advertises *poutargue* among its first courses. Salted, dried grey mullet roes have been a Mediterranean delicacy since the time of the Pharoahs. The Moors probably introduced them to Provence during one of their periodic invasions, and the dish became an established speciality of the coast between Marseille and the Rhône delta, and was sold throughout France. The Rabelaisian hero Grandgousier kept a store of *poutargue* in his loft. The *poutargue* industry was centred on Martigues, but since the war, the mullet catch has dipped dramatically. To compensate for the loss, roes are imported from Mauritania. *Le Bec Fin*'s *poutargue* was actually a kind of taramasalata. Served in a stoneware pot, and flavoured with plenty of basil and cayenne, it was tasty, but it might have raised an eyebrow or two among purists.

As with so many Provençal towns, the central core of Orange seems compressed by the sprawling industrial and residential quarters around it. In 50 years the population has tripled, but it's quite possible to explore the alleys and miniature squares which form the commercial centre during a lazy afternoon stroll. In a lane off the Place des Herbes is a charcuterie, *Aux Trois Petits Cochons*, which cures its own pork and *saucisson sec*. Its dry sausage is without the hint of rancidity which some French pork butchers seem to admire. Better still, it prepares its own *caillettes*, a regional pâté with an authentic Provençal pedigree. According to the patronne of *L'Aigo-Boulido*, who advised me to try them, they are better than those which her husband prepares.

Aux Trois Petits Cochons
5 RUE STASSART
84100 ORANGE
TELEPHONE 90 34 63 58

The word is often written 'gayettes', because it derives from the Provençal for a pig's sweetbreads despite the fact that they are made from liver. One village, Chabeuil in the Drôme, at the northernmost edge of Provence is especially associated with *caillettes*, but they appear on the counters of charcutiers as far south as Aix. They look like old-fashioned English faggots, and the recipe is not so different. Minced liver and pork fat is blended with boiled spinach and flavoured with herbs, before being wrapped in lacy pig's caul and baked. They can be eaten hot, but they are just as good cold when spread in a thick, smooth layer on bread.

That is how I ate mine at the bus terminus in Orange's Place Pourtoules on an October afternoon. The first route I had planned to follow was through Tricastin. Once renowned for its muscat wines, Tricastin became one of France's most productive truffle centres for a few generations until farmers reverted to the more certain income guaranteed to them from wine. Logically, I should have set out from Montélimar and headed straight down the autoroute which runs parallel to the Rhône to St Paul-Trois-Châteaux, the region's capital. But I had decided to cut across country from Orange instead, and set off north-east through the Côtes du Rhône vineyards to Valréas.

There is no one season when Provence outshines, figuratively speaking, the others, but the autumn has a softness which contrasts with the midsummer glare.

Garlic and onions are constant features in Provençal markets and kitchens.

Fresh goat's cheese. Picodon de Valréas has its own appellation contrôlée.

Local wine merchants:

Cellier de l'Enclave des Papes

BP 51

84600 VALREAS

TELEPHONE 90 41 91 42

and

Maison des Vins de l'Union des Vignerons

84600 VALREAS

TELEPHONE 90 37 36 75

The grapes have been harvested, the wine pressed, the vacationers have gone home. The pace of life slows down. Leaves turn copper on the vines, children go back to school and the seasonal hotels, restaurants and gift shops shut. People become more patient, too. The coach driver may offer the lady with no change a free ride. Ask a question at an inquiry desk and you are helped rather than processed.

Valréas has had a complicated history. For the 400 years from the 14th century to the Revolution, it was the administrative centre of a tiny enclave belonging first to the Avignon popes and then to the Vatican. French troops occupied the town in 1791 and, after a referendum, the enclave was annexed by the young French Republic. The town's various communes were split between the *départements* of Drôme and Bouches du Rhône. However, when the previously papal territory of Vaucluse was annexed and created a *département* two years later, Valréas and some neighbouring hamlets opted to join it. Effectively this turned Valréas into an enclave once more, though now a part of France.

Wine growers in the triangle between Grillon, Visan and Valréas have adopted a nominal allegiance to the Holy See, which has allowed them to give the evocative name *Enclave des Papes* to their red Côtes du Rhône. They have a sound historical precedent on their side. John XXII, the second of the Avignon popes, was already an old and sickly man when he was elected in 1316. But he lived to be 89 after undergoing a cure based on liberal doses of Valréas wine. In order to ensure a regular supply, he bought the rights to Valréas which became the Enclave des Papes.

Wines made from grapes grown in the communes of Richerenches, Grillon, Visan and Valréas on 17 domaines may bear the Enclave's escutcheon impressed on the bottle. *Enclave des Papes* should not be confused with another better known wine, *Châteauneuf du Pape*, which comes from vineyards 40 kilometres away. The wines are less powerful than *Châteauneuf du Pape*, but made from the noble Côtes du Rhône grape varieties, Grenache, Cinsault, Syrah and Carignan, they are especially suited to drinking with the local goat's cheese. A bottle from the Valréas co-operative was the most exciting part of my dinner at *La Braserade*, a pretty beamed pizzeria where the cooking was a little disappointing.

I stayed in a room at the *Café de la Paix*, a Belle Epoque relic, which was the social hub of the town's under thirties. It looked like a painting by Van Gogh in one of his more anguished moods: the walls were painted a garish red; the ornate mirror filling the far end of the room had a custard coloured frame. It had a tessellated floor, marble-topped tables, a cane hat stand, billiard table and posters on the wall advertising the claims of pre-war herbal elixirs such as *Origon* and *Magistrale* and a fire-water, *Eau d'Arquebuse*.

I sat at the long J-shaped bar and took up the barmaid's suggestion of a *Châteauneuf du Pape* marc with my coffee. Marc, a spirit made by distilling the compacted residue of pressed grapes, is usually harsh, and requires many years storage in casks before it is ready to drink. This *Réserve des Legats*, was pale amber-tinted marc; smooth, warming and a little like armagnac to sip.

Valréas market
Wednesday

After breakfast the next morning, I found the market in full swing, arching out through the narrow streets off the Place A. Briand. In the South of France, it seems, the older you are, the earlier you start shopping. None of those people crowding around a stall no bigger than a middle-ranking executive's desk at 8 am was under 60 years of age.

Madame Lucienne Hammond specializes in goat's cheeses. The discs of cheese are stacked on bamboo racks in a wooden food safe, some fresh, some shrivelled, some dressed in savory or crushed-peppercorn mackintoshes. She also keeps a large terracotta crock to one side in which her strong-smelling slightly fermented cheese is stored separately.

Picodon de Valréas is listed as a distinct variety of cheese. It's soft and semi-soft as opposed to the Picodon de Dieulefit, which is similar-sized, but older and sharper. A third version of the Picodon was described by Provence's Romantic poet Frédéric Mistral as being left to soak in a vinegar brine for a week. 'With a bit no bigger than an almond,' he wrote, 'you will have enough for a small loaf.'

Madame Hammond's fresh Picodons have a similar style to any fresh goat's cheese except that they have a faint hint of wild herbs. Those from her crock, riper cheeses which have been washed in alcohol, have a sticky rind, are pungent and almost springy to the touch. Following the practised eyes of customers searching out the exact cheese to suit their tastes; watching the patient, cheerful guidance of the lady herself who squeezes every piece she sells to check its texture before wrapping it in waxed paper, is like watching a ritual act, part conspiracy and part chess.

It's the unpredictability, the life in the unpasteurized cheese, which makes it so mysterious. *Affinage*, the process of handling cheese from the time the curdled whey has been formed until the fresh or mature cheeses are eaten is rather like husbandry. No two pieces mature at exactly the same rate, or in the same way.

By coincidence, the morning's papers had carried a story of six *Figaro* journalists poisoned by eating unpasteurized Vacherin cheese. In anywhere but France hygiene propagandists would have been crying out for a ban on all 'raw' (unpasteurized) milk. But the French will never support a national crusade to remove unpasteurized dairy produce – it always fetches a high price in shops and markets. And the Ministry of Agriculture actively supports unpasteurized milk, specifying its use in some of the best-loved cheese and butters which are entitled to an *Appellation d'Origine Contrôlée (AOC)* endorsement in the same way as many wines.

Crediting wine, poultry or cheese with an AOC label (Picodon has one) provides an incentive for small-scale farmers to keep faith with and protect their agricultural heritage, but it can also give the stimulus to a new initiative. The Coteaux de Tricastin wine producing area, centred on the village of Grignan about ten kilometres from Valréas, is one of the smaller and younger members of the AOC club.

In the mid-19th century Tricastin had been a renowned vine-growing area; until a small aphid, *phylloxera vastratix*, crossed the Atlantic and devastated all the European vines by attacking the roots. To replace their cash crop, landowning peasants in the Tricastin area turned to truffles, for which there was an international demand. These 'black diamonds', a kind of subterranean fungus, have a symbiotic relationship with oak trees, so the farmers' first step was to replant the ravaged vineyards with oaks.

Tricastin became a prolific supplier of truffles, but they were an unreliable source of income. They grew wild, they could not be cultivated as such, and the crop varied greatly from year to year. The area still produces most of the truffles grown in France, but between the Wars farmers started to rip up the oak groves and plant vine stocks. At first, the wines were modest, typical of the Côtes du Rhône, but in 1973 a group negotiated the *appellation* and their quality has continued to improve.

Madame Monteillet and her dog go truffle hunting.

Local wine merchants:

Caveau de Grignan
26230 GRIGNAN
TELEPHONE 75 46 55 54

and

Syndicat des Vignerons des Coteaux du Tricastin
MAIRIE DE
ST PAUL-TROIS-CHATEAUX
26130

Domaine de Montine
M. MONTEILLET
GAEC DE LA GRANDE TUILIERE
26230 GRIGNAN
TELEPHONE 75 46 50 51

Since the region produces no more than a handful of wines, it is possible to gain a familiarity with their style from a single tasting. Jean-Luc, son of the Coteaux de Tricastin's president, Roger Monteillet shepherded me through a tasting at the *caves de dégustation* in Grignan where samples from all the wine-makers are kept. Tricastin is lucky in having a *Université du Vin* on its border at Suze-la-Rousse and receives considerable advice from the university's oenologists. The red wines are young, full-bodied and not meant for keeping. The local co-operative's *Chêne Truffier*, 'Truffle Oak', brand contains a large proportion of the Syrah grape, which gives it a pronounced flavour of currants and raspberries. *Domaine de Grangeneuve* vinifies a single grape variety, Syrah. *Domaine de Montine*, the Monteillet's wine is a blend of Grenache, Syrah and Cinsault, and is very like the wine from the *Enclave des Papes* – 'nervous' and tasting of vanilla.

Jean-Luc invited me to visit his father's property, so that I could look at both the vineyard and his family's truffle oak plantations. We drove down a track just outside Grignan on the Valréas road and bumped our way along the domaine's scarred and scalloped slopes. The flat façade of Grignan's château lay like a chocolate-box picture between the horizon and the browning vines.

'When my father was a boy,' Jean-Luc told me, 'he remembers that it was impossible to see from one commune, hamlet or village to the next over the tops of the trees.' Most of the truffle oaks had been hacked down or uprooted, but the family kept a few rows of young trees, planted five metres apart with stripes of lavender bushes growing between them. A few of the older trees lay untended in tangled overgrown coppices, abandoned because truffles no longer grew among their roots.

The Monteillet winery fills the shell of an old staging post. Inside it are rows of stainless steel vats. Roger makes two types of Tricastin wine; the one I had tasted earlier, and another conditioned in oak barrels. He also keeps a no-nonsense Côtes du Rhône wine on tap, and anyone who turns up with a flagon or demijohn can buy it for about seven francs a litre.

Over lunch in the farmhouse, he told me why the truffles had ceased to be a viable commodity, even though they fetch three or four thousand francs per kilo. Truffles cannot be tamed, and they are slow starters. If a farmer plants a truffle oak in chalky soil, in a location known to yield the precious 'black diamonds', with luck he may be able to start cropping them in 15 to 20 years. Thereafter, the spot may go on supplying them for the next 20 years, after which they peter out. At its peak, around 1900, Tricastin was declaring a production of 200 tons a year – 'declaring' being the operative word, since there has always been a black market, and cash payment is the norm. Grignan archives include record sales to the last Russian Tzar, Nicholas II, and up to 2000 kilos have been known to change hands on market day.

As the old plantations wore out, no-one could afford to risk the 20-year wait without a guarantee that replanting would pay dividends. So farmers switched to grapes, initially for cheap *vin de pays*, but now for a wine with a small but growing reputation. The 22 communes of Tricastin declare less than five tons of truffles each year; gone are the days when farmers' wives could play with recipes which ran: 'Acquire some truffles roughly the size of a potato'.

The Monteillet family has not completely abandoned truffle hunting. Pigs were often used to sniff them out, but most farmers will train a dog by burying truffle scented meat and teaching it to find it. Madame Monteillet motioned to a sleek mongrel curled up asleep under the kitchen table. 'I'm trying to train her at the moment,' Madame told me, 'but she's a lazy bitch and disobedient. The last one I had worked well and I was sorry to lose her.'

To the experienced eye, there are two tell-tale signs that truffles are lurking beneath the surface. One is the spiral of small flies, *mouches aux truffes*, which hover above them, attracted by the aroma. The other is a bald area of dead ground, known as the 'burnt patch'. Few plants, with the exceptions of thyme, juniper, rosemary and fennel, flourish above truffles.

Madame had prepared a truffle omelette for lunch. The proper way of consummating the marriage between eggs and truffles is to beat up the one, add plenty of slices of the other, and leave them to harmonize overnight. That way the egg is impregnated by the truffle's scent, which is far more exciting than its rather cardboard texture.

The truffles, Madame Monteillet admitted, were from the previous season, preserved by bottling. 'I sterilize them,' she described, 'for as short a time as I can, and only once. Those sold to the general public must by law be sterilized twice, and as far as I'm concerned they are not worth having because they have lost most of their flavour.'

Our lunch was a topsy-turvy affair starting with salad, then chips before the omelette, which was followed by pork chops, cheese, fruit and coffee. Afterwards, Monsieur Monteillet offered to drive me to a truffle museum at the village of St Paul-Trois-Chateaux. Laid out on two floors in the village's *Syndicat d'Initiative*, it provides erudite insight into the mysteries of the truffle, the *tuber melanosporum*. Apparently microscopic webs of mycelium form between the tree's roots and are colonized by mycorrhizomes, themselves a kind of fungus, on which the truffles form and which provide the nutrients which help the truffles grow.

I wanted to return to Grignan and look at its château, but there was no bus and no taxi in the village, so I thumbed a ride. A young baker in a battered yellow Citroën gave me a lift. He worked in Montségur and nodded at the *boulangerie* where he worked as he drove past. It bore a sign in large Gothic lettering advertising *Pain aux Courges*, marrow bread.

'Do you have the recipe?' I asked.

'I'm just an employee' he hedged. 'I don't know the proportions.'

'What kind of a bread is it?'

'Do you know what a *pâte aux pognes* is? It's like brioche: eggs, salt, strong flour and yeast. You make a dough and then you put in the marrow.'

'Raw?'

'A purée that has been cooked and dried.'

More than that he was not prepared to divulge. I never tasted his bread, and I never saw it anywhere else, though I have found plenty of *pognes* made into the shape of crowns, especially in the Vaucluse and Drôme.

My chauffeur-boulanger dropped me in Grignan by the statue of Madame de Sévigné. One of the great, fashionable beauties of Louis XIV's reign, she owes her literary fame to the intense, affectionate letters which she wrote to her daughter, Francoise-Marguerite, who married the Comte de Grignan, then Governor of Provence. Mme de Sévigné spent the last months of her life in the château, which is

Lines of lavender point towards the Château de Grignan.

set on an exposed rocky outcrop with the winding streets of the village spun about it. She wrote that when the North wind blew, it whipped up the gravel on the château's terrace and shattered the windows on the second floor.

Mme de Sévigné delighted in the pleasures of her daughter's table. 'These partridges,' she cooed in an epistle to her uncle and confidant, the Abbé de Coulanges, 'are all fed on thyme, marjoram and all the perfumes of our sachets; there is no need to select them. The same is true of the plump quail of which the leg should pull away without a battle (it never fails to), and of the turtle doves, all equally perfect. As for melons, figs and muscat grapes, it's strange, but if we wanted a bad melon by some bizarre fancy, we should have to send to Paris for it; there are none here. The figs are white and sugary, the muscats like crunchable amber seeds. They would turn your head if you went on eating them without moderation, because it's like sipping the most exquisite Saint Laurent wine.'

The castle has been a place of literary pilgrimage since the middle of the 18th century, despite the fact that the Grignan family sold it and all its furnishings to cover their debts. From the outside it seems every bit a palace, surrounded by stone courtyards and balustrades overlooking the spreading Tricastin plain below. But revolutionaries gutted the building, so that few genuine traces of Mme de Sévigné's presence remain, except for the rooms themselves. Unfortunately, they have been furnished in a haphazard way. I wanted to visit the kitchens, but they had been dismantled and converted into a recording studio.

After nightfall, the alleys interlocked around the château are dark and smell of woodsmoke. The temperature drops and barn owls swoop through the space between the rooftops and the silhouetted castle walls. In the silence and shadows, it was easy to conjure up images of the string of messengers bearing letters of delicious gossip about card games, dinners, duels, doctors, priests, money matters, executions, Louis' mistresses, victories and defeats, the death of a marshal of France and, on one occasion, of a *maître d'hôtel.*

L'Eau à la Bouche
MONIQUE LAROCHE
RUE ST-LOUIS
26230 GRIGNAN
TELEPHONE 75 46 57 37

It would have been too much to expect plump partridge for dinner in a village of barely a thousand inhabitants, but I did discover a pretty restaurant, *L'Eau à la Bouche*, with a log fire, bunches of dried flowers hanging from the ceiling and a patronne with the appetising proportions of Mme de Sévigné's statue if not the plunging *décolletage*. She was not a trained restauratrice – few women are in this male-dominated profession – but she had a natural talent for chatting to customers. As the room filled up, she rationed her charms accordingly. She served me a menu of *gratin d'escargots, steak aux poivrons* and a spiced pear which I washed down with a Coteaux de Tricastin. A young Frenchman at a nearby table wanted a bottle of Badoit mineral water rather than wine, and received a little of the patronne's sarcasm along with it: 'Are you bothered about the vintage?', she asked.

BLACK OLIVES AND GARRIGUE WINE

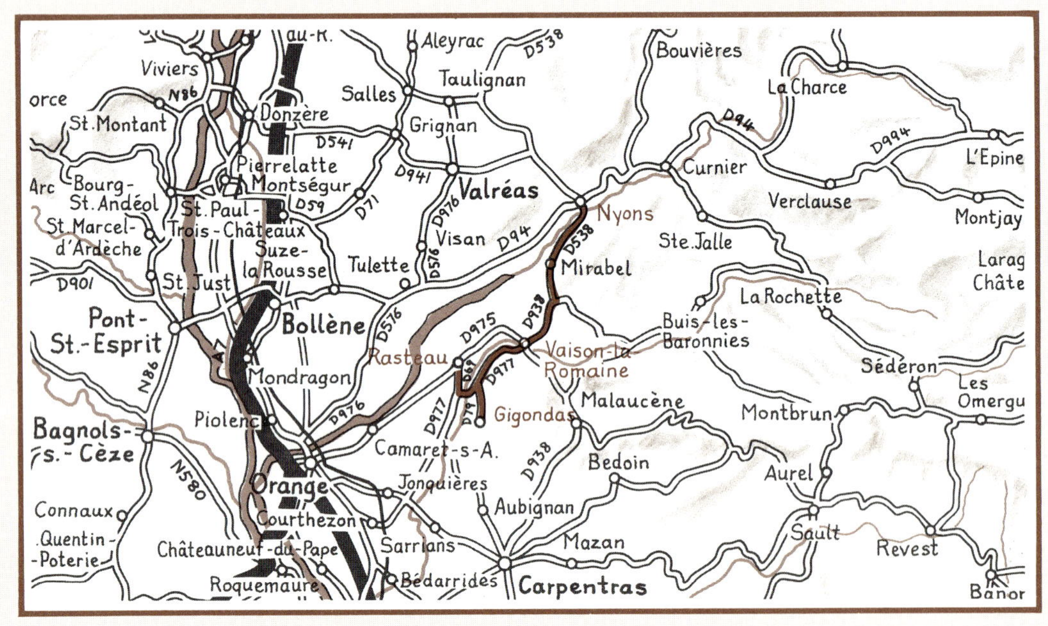

Nyons – Vaison-la-Romaine – Gigondas – Rasteau

Next morning, Thursday, I caught the bus to Nyons. It was only a 40 minute journey (it would be less by car), but the dusky hills, mottled with olive trees starting to brush against the flat or gently undulating fields of reddening autumn vines gave a foretaste of a wilder side to the Provençal landscape.

Olive trees give an impression of permanence but it is something of an illusion. Great frosts in 1956 and again in 1985 have decimated the *olivettes*, the olive groves, and far too few new trees have been replanted to make up the losses. For all that, olive-oil, with wild herbs and garlic remains one of the trinity of flavours which give Provençal food its spirit.

When Madame de Sévigné teased her daughter, writing: 'I cannot feel sorry for your lack of butter, since you have such admirable oil', she was probably referring to an olive-oil similar to the kind still made at Nyons. At the eastern end of the Tricastin plain, Nyons is the centre of an industry built around a single olive variety, the Tanche. Since olive trees can survive upwards of 300 years, it is conceivable that the same trees which supplied the Château de Grignan during the reign of Louis XIV are growing the raw material for Autrand, Ramade, the Huilerie du Pont Roman, the Coopérative Oleicole and other oil mills in and around the town.

The finest oils are rare and twice as expensive as butter. As with wine, a glimpse at the label on a bottle goes some way to telling what the contents are. *Vierge*, or virgin oil, must be unadulterated olive juice, obtained by crushing and pressing the fruit without heating it. This 'cold pressed oil' has three grades: *extra, fine* and *semi-fine*, reflecting its acidity. The more acidic it is, the more likely the oil is to turn rancid. 'Pure' olive-oil is a blend of deodorized, refined oil with a little virgin oil added for flavour. Cakes of pressed olives, known as *grignons*, can be chemically treated with water and solvents and repressed to give an extraction known as *huile de grignons*, but this is normally used only for animal feed.

Telling virgin oils apart is really an esoteric skill mastered by a handful of experts, but there are simple ground rules for choosing them. A major brand's oil always has the same taste and texture, because it will have been blended to achieve a reliable standard. Smaller independent oil mills each create a style which reflects

J. Ramade
AVENUE PAUL LAURENS
26110 NYONS
TELEPHONE 75 26 08 18

Nyons market
Thursday

the variety of the olives, the local preferences, the judgement of the miller and even the climate. As with wines, there are good years and bad. Every year there are competitions held in Draguignan and Nice to assess the best oils, and there is no guarantee that a mill which wins a gold medal for its product one year will receive the same accolade the next.

The Tanche, the olive for which Nyons is renowned, is medium sized and heart shaped. It yields an old-bronze tinted oil very different from the chartreuse-green oils pressed some 60 kilometres south in the mills at Fontvieille and in the Vallée des Baux. The colour reflects the fruit's ripeness, or slight overripeness in the Tanche's case. Harvesting starts in December when the olives have turned black. Washed and graded, they are crushed and pulped by a millstone before pressing. The extracted oil is separated from the water in the fruit by a filter or a centrifugal machine.

Until recent times, the pulp was scooped on to thick coconut mats, *scourtins*, before pressing, but these have been supplanted by nylon sheets and the coconut versions, dyed in bright colours are sold as doormats.

The smaller mills may produce several sorts of virgin oil. Moulin J. Ramade, down a narrow street close to the Nyons Co-operative has a thicker, darker oil and a more fluid, fruity one. Because taste is such a subjective thing, it pays to try out as many kinds as possible. Some small peasant farmers still press their own olives and bring their surplus into Nyons to sell at the Thursday market in dubious-looking litre bottles. Some of these survivors of old Provence still continue the tradition of dunking bread into the oil as it comes off the press and roasting the slices over a wood fire. These *roustidos* can be less enjoyable than they sound because raw olives contain a bitter glucoside, *oleuropein*, which has an astringent, lip-numbing effect. It's not present in the oil after separation, but can provide an unpleasant surprise if filtering is not perfect.

The Tanche is a favourite olive for eating with an aperitif. Once it has been cured, it has a wrinkled skin, a bit like an undersized prune, which makes it quite distinct from the other black table olive found in the South of France, the small, smooth Cailletier. Like Picodon cheese or Tricastin wine, Nyons oil and the olives have their own *appellation contrôlée*.

Many families wait for the first frosts before picking or purchasing the ripest most wrinkled olives they can find and salt them themselves. They prick the skins with a needle or a sharp tined fork and bury the olives in a crock containing sea salt and pepper. Every day the crock is shaken and extra seasoning added until, at the end of a few days, their natural astringency has gone and they are ready for eating.

Monsieur Ropar, who farms at St Ferreol Trente Pas, a hamlet in the hills just north of Nyons, sells home-cured Tanches in the town's market, either on their own or flavoured with garlic and with herbs. He stocks that other stand-by of the Provençal pickle drum, *olives cassées* – broken olives. Broken olives are made from a small pointed variety, the Picholine, which is picked green at the end of the summer. The surface of the fruit is bruised and split by a blow with a wooden hammer or rolling pin and the olives are left to soak in water, which must be changed every day, for over a week. Then they are drowned in a brine flavoured with fennel, dried orange peel and any other aromatic plants which may appeal to the cook. After a few days steeping they are ready to eat.

M. Ropar
LES CONDAMINES
ST FERREOL TRENTE PAS
26110 NYONS
TELEPHONE 75 27 72 24

Nyons market sprawls across the Place de la Libération before boring into the leading edge of the medieval streets. Its axis is a mobile pizzeria, a battered grey Citroën van with a wood-fired oven behind the driver's seat and a counter along one side. Pizza popularity has reached epidemic proportions in Provence, which is only a good or bad thing in so far as the pizzas are tasty or not. Here, a permanent queue stretched back beyond the man handing out samples of Ardèche *saucisson* on the neighbouring stall.

It's tempting to imagine the stallholders with their trestle tables and awnings as a modern nomadic tribe flitting from town to town setting up their wares early in the morning and dismantling them at midday before moving on. Some do fit that description, but there are many others who bring their own surplus produce to sell, a few cheeses whenever they happen to be in season, eggs, honey, flowers, vegetables or a dozen chickens still alive and clucking in portable cages.

I spent a leisurely hour putting together the basis for an impromptu picnic. From the Moulin Ramade, I bought a jar of *tapénade*, a paste of black olives, oil and capers. In a bakery near the post office, I found a small *pogne* which reminded me of the baker from Montségur. Sausage, pizza, tomato, peppery Tanches, Ardechois bread and a bottle of Côtes du Rhône from SCAN (the Société Coopérative Agricole du Nyonsais) completed the bill of fare. With these I climbed up through the tunnelled gallery of the Rue des Grands Forts towards the Quartier des Forts, a jumble of anarchically sited houses built among the rocks and ruins of the old citadel. Part of the way I followed a small tractor pulling a trailer of rocks for repairing gaps in bulging garden walls; it knocked out even more stones when it tried to negotiate the tight turnings in the narrow passageways.

The steep path led upwards to the Tour Randonne, a crenellated tower decorated with ornamental buttresses and the statue of the Virgin perched on top of them. Though it looks like a Gothic folly, it houses a tiny 13th-century chapel dedicated to Notre Dame de Bon Secours. From this vantage point is a view of Les Baronnies, the interlocking range of hills in whose fertile, sheltered valleys many of the *olivettes* grow. I lunched on a patch of ground under a fig tree overhanging a garden fence and planned out the next stage of my route.

Nyons is at a natural crossroads with fingers pointing through the Eygues Valley towards Gap, across the Tricastin plain and south towards Carpentras. In the early siesta part of the afternoon, I crossed the Eygues and started walking towards Vaison-La-Romaine.

A young mother who had just dropped her daughter with a baby-sitter and was taking the afternoon off to go climbing in the hills stopped to give me a lift. She was a Parisian emigré with a job making plaster mouldings, bunches of grapes, curlicues and typical motifs to decorate renovated Provençal homes. With Paris only an hour's flight away, old farm houses, the *mas*, were in great demand as weekend or holiday homes and there was no shortage of work for her.

Because the road was blocked by a truck, she had to double back towards Nyons and make for Vaison across country through olive groves. French farmers do not amass fortunes from these plantations which are often pocket handkerchiefs compared to those in Spain or Italy. After the deadly frosts, few new trees have been replanted and those which have been will take several generations to mature before they can be cropped. Some peasants have been tempted to claim subsidies on trees which no

Shimmering olive trees on the slopes around Nyons.

Lou Canésteou
NICOLE DEJOUX
10 RUE RASPAIL
84110 VAISON-LA-ROMAINE
TELEPHONE 90 36 31 30

longer exist. There is no risk that the olive will ever die out in Provence, but except in specific regions such as Nyons, it no longer enjoys the privileged economic position which it once had.

Vaison-La-Romaine has fewer inhabitants than Nyons, but it seems far grander because it is effectively towns from three separate eras stitched to form a loosely fitting whole. The Roman city, excavated on sites several acres across fills two dusty cavities at its northern boundary. Next to it is the thriving modern town. Across the River Ouvèze, linked by a single-span bridge built by legionnaires, is the medieval acropolis which was abandoned during the 18th century and restored as a comfortable suburb for the local bourgeois.

One reason why Vaison-la-Romaine appears so prosperous is that it is surrounded by a clutch of villages eminent for the wine they produce: Rasteau, Beaumes-de-Venise, Vacqueyras and Gigondas. Bottles of these and other Côtes du Rhône vintages line one wall of an appropriately refined cheese shop, *Lou Canestéou*, by the Place Montfort. Here, trays and counters are overrun with Picodons, Peahans, Banons and Valréas cheeses. Nicole Dejoux, the owner, also keeps a bin behind the counter in which she ferments her own home-brewed *cachat*. This overpowering blend of ripe cheeses was once given to servants on the farms where nothing went to waste.

To concoct it, she needs a starter, an old blue cheese of the roquefort type which acts like a 'mother of vinegar'. On to that she throws pepper, *eau de vie* and the old goat's cheese which she works in by hand to form an edible putty. Its taste hits you in the mouth like well-placed combination punches. The first blow is a sense of chewing putrefying Stilton which, considering the fabrication, is not far off what it is. Phase two is a period of prickly heat titillating the tastebuds. Lastly, well after the *cachat* has started its minuet with the gastric juices, comes a long – and if you still have an open mind – pleasing, almost sweet back taste.

Madame Dejoux recommended it on toast with aperitifs, but that is a reflection on the kind of business she runs. I could imagine scraping it over a slab of bread while sitting on top of Mont Ventoux and swilling from a jug of the roughest rosé between mouthfuls.

Strangely, for a lady who will roll up her sleeves and plunge her arms into a mass of living bacteria, Madame Dejoux does not like foreign fingers tampering with her merchandise. 'The other day,' she admitted 'I got angry with some Dutchmen who were picking up my cheeses. The English,' she added, 'know how to behave.'

While we were talking, a lady came into the shop and Madame Dejoux introduced me. 'This is Madame Joyet,' she said, 'who has a vineyard in Rasteau. She is one of my prized suppliers. This Englishman is interested in wine. Perhaps he would like to look at your property.'

'Would you mind if I visited you?'

'Whenever you like.'

We settled on the following afternoon.

Before I left her shop, Madame Dejoux picked me a Picodon from a full basket under a gauze cloth. 'Look,' she said, 'giving it an educated squeeze, 'this one is just right; that one there is harder. It's still good cheese, but will be drier and sharper.' I took note, but remembered not to touch.

To clear the heady *cachat* fumes, I popped into an excellent patisserie and Salon de Thé, *Lanchier-Avias*. There is nothing remotely Provençal about a teashop, but it is indicative of the way Provence has evolved and outgrown its image as a poor relation of the rest of France that it's possible to find cakes to suit the most demanding self-indulgent palate in a place hardly bigger than a village.

Lanchier-Avias
PLACE MONFORT
84110 VAISON-LA-ROMAINE
TELEPHONE 90 36 09 25

Over a cup of herb tea, I nibbled a chocolate mousse, coffee cream and sponge structure seven layers deep which was as satisfyingly sticky as it was light. Then, because of the regional link, I tucked into a cup cake studded with the pine kernels. Pine kernels have been used for Provençal sweetmeats for at least four centuries. Nostradamus, the 16th-century astrologer, who was born in St Rémy-de-Provence, even wrote down a recipe for a pine-kernel biscuit which he called *pignoulat*. In fact, he gives both a summer and a winter version.

I wanted a room for the night and booked one at the *Hostellerie les Florets* at Gigondas. The choice was not entirely random, because it belongs to a consortium, *Hostellerie du Vignoble Français*, whose members, small family-run hotels, must be located in a wine producing region and serve regional food and wine.

Hostellerie les Florets
84190 GIGONDAS
TELEPHONE 90 65 85 01

The taxi driver who drove me there admitted that he was not a connoisseur, but he was going to a Côtes du Rhône wine fair, held at the Auchan Hypermarché in Avignon where he hoped he would be able to pick up a few bargains. In his job, it did not pay to be over-fond of wine, especially the heavy red Gigondas.

Les Florets was on a side road leading to the Dentelles de Montmirail, a sharp-toothed granite ridge which overhangs the walled village of Gigondas. A hotel like this, planted between the rocks, vines and wilderness owes its survival to the wine-bibbers who visit the village. The Bernard family which owns the hotel is one of the region's major growers of Vacqueyras and Gigondas wines.

The rooms, furnishings, even service here are subservient to the restaurant wine list. It carries nearly all the Gigondas growths like a roll of honour: Amadieu, Archimbaud, Ay Dominique, Bernard, Beaumont, Beaumet, Boutière, Cartier, Chapalain, Chauvet, Cave des Vignerons, Croset, Cuillerat, Faraud, Gaudin, Gorecki, Meffre R, Meffre S, Richard, Roux, Saurel, Vache. In late autumn, when the bedrooms are unlet and the waiter doubles as concierge and the modest public room seems several sizes too large, the names strike the imagination like so many genies sealed away in bottles.

When the corks come out, they can turn heads. Madame Bernard, who is in charge of the hotel, mentioned that she had had a visit from a journalist on a British wine magazine who stayed in the hotel a little while before. He had carried out an impromptu tasting. 'He appeared to know what he was doing,' Madame allowed herself a faint trace of scepticism. He had decanted some bottles, emptied the contents of one glass into another to oxygenate the wines and tried the wine at different temperatures. 'Did it make a difference?' I asked. 'He seemed to think so.' 'And what would you do?' 'Except when it is very old, we would open the bottle about a quarter of an hour before starting to drink it.'

If Madame felt vaguely amused by the palaver of an Anglo-Saxon, she feared the power and influence of the French gastronomic press. Figuratively speaking, a wine and food magazine has a restaurant over a barrel. 'They say,' Madame Bernard lamented, naming no names 'they are going to write a review about us and afterwards they invite us to advertise with them.'

After unpacking, I settled down in the corner of the bar with a bottle of white

The Tanche, Nyons' black olive.

Vacqueyras and a dish of wrinkled Tanches. Some had a persistent garlic taste and a pleasing hint of bitterness. Others were lightly flavoured with chilli. They enhanced the fruity Vacqueyras which is made from Clairette grapes, a variety often disregarded by wine masters in the know because it goes into so much *vin ordinaire*, but on the right soil and when carefully vinified, it can make a white wine as good in its way as the highly rated Vacqueyras reds.

Dinner kicked off with a smooth truffle-flecked thrush pâté in a white porcelain pot. It's illegal to shoot thrushes, but they remain an arch enemy of wine growers because the birds plunder the grapes. To avoid any direct confrontation with the law, menus advertise 'Bird pâté' and leave diners to draw the obvious inference. *Les Florets* puts nothing in writing, but delivers the smooth faintly gamey paste as a little something extra to whet the appetite. The big slightly peppery Gigondas, Domaine 'La Garrigue', which the Bernard family produces slid down a treat with it.

A salad with warm pheasant breasts, livened up by wild mushrooms and crisp *flûtes* of fried bread spread with a red pepper purée followed. It was not really a 'Chartreuse' as the menu described it. Without wishing to sound a know-all, I doubt whether many restaurants still make this classic dish – a pheasant, sausage and cabbage stew which is simmered in broth and pressed into a mould lined with vegetables. Borrowing traditional titles for new creations is one of Nouvelle Cuisine's minor aberrations, but it was a pity to find this in a restaurant priding itself on its uncomplicated regional dishes.

The main course, *Pieds et paquets*, feet and packages, is part and parcel of the real Provençal repertoire. Pigs', or more often sheeps' tripe and sometimes ears are stewed overnight, together with trotters. Marseille is credited with inventing the dish, and a ditty ties it to the suburb of La Pomme on the eastern edge of the city:

Allons à la Pomme
Manger les paquets
Et nous ferons comme
Les Marseillais.

(Let's go to La Pomme and eat *paquets*. And we'll be acting like the Marseillais.)

At *Les Florets*, the ears and tripe, stuffed with pork, garlic and herbs, were tender enough to cut with a fork. The trotter had given the wine sauce a gelatinous body which clung to the lips like lip-salve. *Pieds et paquets* is one of those slow-cooked dishes which taste better when reheated. This had been, and the flavours of meat, thyme, wine and tomato had amalgamated to leave a long memorable taste. It was not refined cooking, but it had the authority of a recipe which had been cooked over and over again. As a partner to the Gigondas it was ideal, making the wine seem richer and longer, smoothing away its tannic edge.

For cheese I had a large piece of Banon. It's often exported as a small disc wrapped in vine leaves tied with raffia, but the genuine article, made from goat's milk, is prepared by farms on the slopes of Mont Ventoux. The fresh cheeses are left to dry in the dairy for a month before being packed for sale into brown, chestnut-leaf parcels.

Early next morning, I breakfasted under the plane trees on the hotel terrace. Looking up at the Dentelles de Montmirail, I could not help feeling that they have been misnamed. The word *dentelles* signifies lace. To me the crenated rocks seem menacing rather than frilly and tame. They emerge jagged from the *garrigue*, the wooded, tangled, stony slopes, thick with broom and thistles which grow right up to the Gigondas and neighbouring Vacqueyras vineyards.

I set out to amble the dozen or so miles to Rasteau to meet the Joyets. On foot, the landscape takes on a different identity from the scenery glimpsed through a passing car window. Little clumps of thyme, the flecks of dry leaves set out in pairs among the straggly stalks, dot the roadside and a few yards further back into the undergrowth the slightly larger, spear-leafed savory and lusher marjoram flourish on the stone soil. Dun-capped *boletus* mushrooms, *cèpes*, with their spongy underbellies pop out of the leaf litter.

I met a man with a basketful who had parked his car in a lay-by between Gigondas and Sablet. He said that he picked them early in the morning before the worms could attack them. *Cèpes*, he told me, are among the best edible fungi, but they require long cooking as a safety measure because one of the parasites which burrows into them will attack the human liver if not destroyed by heat.

Domaine des Girasols

PAUL JOYET

RASTEAU

84110 VAISON-LA-ROMAINE

TELEPHONE 90 46 11 70

A lane skirting the village of Sablet crosses the River Ouvèze, its low-slung banks scuffed with untended vines, olives and almond trees, and hits the road to Rasteau. It's not a spectacular village like Gordes, Roussillon or even Séguret across the river, which is perched on a knoll with the Dentelles de Montmirail at its back. But there is a pervasive yeasty fume, which gives it the unmistakable character of a wine centre. It used to be noted for its sweet white wines made from Muscat grapes and slightly fortified, but its supremacy has been challenged by the luscious, scented Beaumes-de-Venise.

Because I was early for my meeting, I drank a chilled, acidic rosé at the bar of the café overlooking the square. The family midday meal was in progress. Two tables had been pushed together and a whole poached hake lay on a stainless steel flat with dishes of potatoes, green beans, carrots and a thick-cut tomato salad around it. All that was missing to make it a feast was a bowl of the velvety, garlic perfumed mayonnaise, *aïoli*. It was hard not to experience a pang of envy as well as hunger as I watched four generations picking the fish clean, even scooping out the almonds of white flesh from the fish's cheeks.

Les Girasols, Monsieur and Madame Paul Joyet's property spreads over 30 acres of undulating, south-facing hills on the edge of Rasteau. They chose the name because the Girasol is both a sunflower which turns to face the sun like their vines, and a kind of golden brown opal which reminded them of the smooth pebbles which cover the soil. Paul Joyet, until ten years ago, had been a market gardener outside Lyon. He had built up a business selling vegetables to the starred restaurants in and around France's gastronomic mecca. At the back of his mind he had always wanted to switch from carrots and turnips to vines, and when the opportunity of buying Les Girasols occurred he snapped it up.

Tending vines and making wine require infinite pains and attention to detail more than technical skills. What the Joyets lacked in experience they compensated for with their enthusiasm. They had also picked an especially favourable site. It's a basic fact that older vines tend to give finer wine. Each plot on the domaine has its name and history. Tombaronne, the oldest, was planted in 1905. Labrune dates from 1914. It's Monsieur Paul's favourite, and produces grapes which always contribute

A winter vineyard near Sablet, and the jagged Dentelles de Montmirail.

to his most successful vintages. Two other plots – Malalangue and Lampreuse – were started soon after the Great War. The combination of old stock and clay soil strewn with limestone pebbles creates a sympathetic environment which Monsieur Paul swiftly learnt how to harness.

Although Rasteau has its own *appellation contrôlée*, and its reputation is based on the Muscat wines, it falls, as do Gigondas and Coteaux de Tricastin, within the Côtes du Rhône mainframe. *Domaine des Girasols* makes outstanding red wines of this type. Monsieur Paul argued that two steps in the process had a special bearing on the quality of his wine: the *assemblage*, the selection of grapes which are blended to make his wines, and their vinification. He aims at a varietal cocktail of 60 per cent Grenache, 30 percent Cinsault and the balance split between Mourvèdre and Carignan, but the choice of grapes from the better, usually the older plots will also affect quality. The proportions are determined in advance, so that the precise amounts are picked and emptied into the vat on the same day, precluding the need for any blending later on. Although he has learnt quickly and trusts his own judgement, he consults a professional oenologist at critical moments, such as the vendange – when the grapes are harvested.

The vinification of his red wines, the process when the juice ferments and becomes wine, is achieved by gravity. The vat is filled with unpressed grapes which are passed through a screw which splits them without reducing them to pulp. The juice is extracted by the natural pressure of the grapes causing the stalks and skins to rise as the fermentation takes place. Once the juice has vinified, it is drawn off into storage vats and eventually casks. It's a technique producing wine which is ready to drink after a couple of years, but with good keeping qualities.

Therein lies the difficulty for many of the young generation of Provençal growers. They have to turn over their stock while the wines are still young in order to repay the money they owe the bank, knowing that they could become much better and more valuable given the chance. Monsieur Paul has kept a few hundred bottles of his 1983 vintage in reserve, a wine which is still sparkling bright and with a long finish. He called it 'Savage' with a mixture of respect and affection, in recognition of the fact that the wine had an unpredictable life of its own.

Describing a wine's taste can sound artificial even when it is being precise. James Thurber mocked 'the naïve little domestic Burgundy – but I think you'll be amused by its pretentions' school of commentary to perfection. Monsieur Paul sprang a definition on me which did not register at first. He said the characteristic flavour of his wine was of a Berlingot de Carpentras. 'What's that?' I asked. 'Oh! a *bonbon Anglais.*' By that, it transpired, he meant a 'boiled sweet' – something between a humbug and barley sugar. It would have been easy to be wise after the event and agree with him. Instead, I told him what I thought – that his Côtes du Rhône was the best I had ever tasted.

3

QUINCE BREAD FOR BREAKFAST

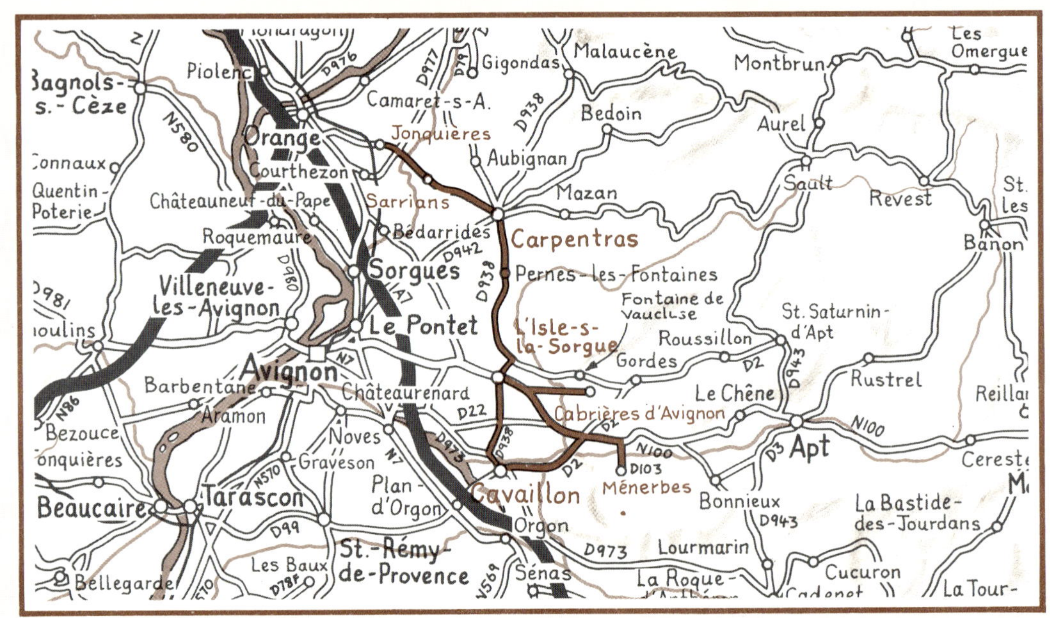

Jonquières – Sarrians – Carpentras – Cavaillon – Ménerbes – L'Isle-sur-la-Sorgue – Cabrières d'Avignon

Dangling a trio of bottles from Monsieur Paul over one arm and my travelling grip over the other, I reached Jonquières after dark. From there I hoped to bus or train my way into Carpentras, but the railway line passing through the village only handles freight and there was no other public transport. The only hotel open gave me a room, but refused to feed me on the grounds that it was throwing a party for the members of the local football team.

I paid in advance, drank a beer and turned in. Next morning at half-past six I attempted to leave, but all the doors were locked. I tried to escape via the kitchen and finished in a locked garage. The door to the café was barred so I went in search of a manager or night watchman. At the end of a passage on the first floor I knocked on an unnumbered door. It looked promising because a couple of pairs of well-worn flat-heeled shoes, the kind waitresses wear, lay outside it. It was a good guess. A bleary-eyed girl in a nightdress opened up and asked me what I wanted. To be let out. No, she could not do that because she did not have the keys. She only slept there. The boss usually opened the café at seven.

And so he did. No bus was leaving or due to leave for Carpentras, so I hitched a ride from a Moroccan mechanic who worked in the neighbouring village of Sarrians. He advised me to drop in at the bakery before continuing my journey. It was up a side-street, a three-storey building with a stack of logs piled almost up to the shuttered first floor windows outside it. It had no shop front, but the warm scent of baking wafted into the small square of which it formed one side.

Inside, an assortment of bread lay on a wooden table which served as a counter, not the cloned torpedoes of the modern boulangerie, nor even the convex slabs of *pain de campagne*, but dusty, irregular shaped loaves, crisp *fougasses* – savoury flat breads with gashes through the middle – and a few croissants rolled as neatly as cigars. What caught my eye were three dumpy pasties and the handwritten label next to them, *pain aux coings*, quince bread. A pretty girl in a track-suit bottom and trainers wrapped one for me and I left to eat it outside. It was still hot in the hand. I parked myself on the pavement opposite from where I could watch the baker at work and started to breakfast.

Marius Dumas

PORTE D'AMONT

84260 SARRIANS

TELEPHONE 90 65 42 15

I have never come across 'quince bread' anywhere except in Sarrians. The outside was no more than bread dough, thick enough to contain the fruit but not so thick as to be stodgy. Inside, was a halved quince, sweet and just cooked through. Quinces were once among the most popular fruit. In the Middle Ages they were an essential ingredient of the English apple pie, giving it a perfumed flavour that no apple alone can match. But they fell from grace, because they are astringent when eaten raw. Agro-Industry finds it more profitable to grow Le Crunch, the Golden-Not-So-Delicious apple than a fruit which requires a minimal amount of effort to be spent on it before it yields its virtue.

In southern France, quinces are still cultivated on a small scale, mainly for the older generation with time enough to prepare jellies. In the Provençal village of Fontvieille near Arles, I once chatted to a elderly lady sitting outside a dark courtyard with a bucket of quinces and their peelings. She explained that she had picked them from trees which grew wild thereabouts and was going to prepare a 'marmelade' with them. It may have been an acidental choice of words, *marmelade* in French can refer to any sweetened purée of fruit, but it derives from the Spanish *marmelada* – quince jam. Cotignac, a village in the Var, actually translates as 'quince jam'.

One of the bakers must have noticed me watching, because the girl called to me and invited me inside. Two men shared the work, one of them preparing the dough, the other plying the oven. Both wore shorts and tennis shirts to keep cool in the stifling atmosphere. Their shift had began the previous evening at 10.30 pm and they were carrying on until after nine.

The building's shell dated from the last century, but the oven was at least a couple of hundred years older. It was constructed of stone blocks shaped to all intents and purposes like the top of an igloo and about two metres across. A sign above its blackened cast iron doors admonished '*Défense de Fumer*', No Smoking, but when the split logs were pushed through the gate on to the oven floor they spewed a gale of burning charcoal smoke into the bakery which would have annihilated any trace of a surreptitious cigarette.

There was no need to light the wood; it was blazing within seconds. The sooty fumes did not last long and when the flames burned clear, the baker took a pole with a hook like a bishop's mitre or a Roman strigil on the end of it and scraped the red-hot cinders to one side. The oven temperature used for baking bread was somewhere between 300°C and 400°C, hotter than the hottest pizza ovens.

The standard loaves baked at Sarrians are called *Pains de Beaucaire* after the town on the Rhône not far from Avignon. It's an attribution going back centuries and no diligent bread-hunter would find anything as authentic as the Sarrians bread in modern-day Beaucaire. It's made with leaven rather than the usual brewer's yeast and has a denser texture than the over-aerated baguettes. The trick is in the kneading and the shaping. The trough in which the dough was once pummelled is still there, but the baker recently, that is about 50 years ago, switched to a bowl with electrically powered paddles for mixing the flour, yeast and water to the proper elasticity. This tool is unlike modern mixing bowls which wrench the dough into shape in a few minutes. Each batch is cut and turned and folded for an hour before it is ready.

The secret of *Pain de Beaucaire* is in its shape. The soft dough is rolled out by hand into sheets about two metres long, folded in half across the short side and laid out into wooden boxes. It's dusted with a flour made from ground olive stones. 'We wonder,' the baker told me, 'whether it can really be that, but sometimes we get it in our eyes and it does not swell like it would if it were only flour.' Unlike modern doughs, it does not need to develop or double its size before baking, but the dough is cut and turned on its side so that the fold is uppermost.

Because of the extreme heat, loading the bread in the oven, baking it and extracting it is carried out as a single, infernal rotation of tasks. The baker puts four unbaked loaves on to an elongated peel, shaking them out on to the oven floor. Constantly under pressure, he fills the oven as fast as he can. When the last of the batch goes in, the first ones are ready to come out. The baked loaves which are lying closest to the ashes rise the most. Those furthest away are more compact. Any trimmings are fashioned into *tourtes* and *fougasses* and baked at odd moments.

This technique has probably not changed since the oven was first built. It demands tremendous stamina from the bakers. The two commis were both rugbymen and said they thrived on the draining heat. Marius Dumas, the owner of the bakery, had taught them their craft, but he no longer worked nights. They showed me a

The bakery at Sarrians, where traditional Pain de Beaucaire *is baked* au bois.

Some of the bakery's other specialities.

press cutting of him visiting Japan to teach his skills in a cookery school. No way, they insisted, would the Japanese ever bake bread like the Sarrians bakery.

The peel with which the baker shovelled his loaves in and out of the oven has a narrow blade about two feet long and a handle taller than a man. A Provençal folk tale tells how a sailor from Marseille decided to give up the sea. He headed inland with his knapsack tied around an old oar. In every village where he stopped, he made love to the prettiest girl he could find and afterwards popped the question: 'What's this?' showing her his oar. And every time the answer came back: 'That's an oar.'

After many weeks, when he was far, far away from the coast, he arrived in the village where there was a particularly buxom wench who appeared rather stupid. The sailor followed his habitual procedure, he was becoming an expert, and soon won her over. When he asked about the oar, she replied: 'Why, that's a bread peel, of course. Everybody knows that.' The sailor knew that he had escaped far enough from the sea, so he proposed to the girl, she accepted, they were married and they settled down in the village.

About a year later, the sailor thought he would explain his stratagem to his wife. 'Remember when I first met you?' he asked. 'Of course,' she replied. 'You tried to fool me with that oar of yours, but I knew what you were up to. I thought, you're good looking enough, and it's about time that I find a husband, so why not play along with it.'

The bus from Sarrians to Carpentras was special in one detail. The only Frenchman on it was the driver. Nearly all the passengers came from North Africa. The tourist holidaying in Provence may not notice them, since he is rubbing shoulders with others of his kind, but out of season, Moroccans, Algerians and Tunisians, employed as cheap labour in the fields and packing stations, are everywhere.

Monsieur Le Pen, the right-wing politician, owes his power base in Provence in general and in Marseille in particular to the fact that he can point a finger in any direction and home in on an immigrant face. What he chooses to forget is that Marseille itself was a colony founded by Phocian Greeks from Asia Minor.

Carpentras' cathedral wall was smeared with an ironic nationalist jibe. Printed in a black hexagon were four words: 'Couscous, Paella, Kouglof, Mmm!' Had the graffiti artist added pizza to that list, he would have had a stronger case to argue. Rabid chauvinism is particularly misplaced in a town like Carpentras since it used to be capital of the Comtat de Venaissin, a papal dominion for 500 years and did not become a part of France until the Revolution.

The town is at the epicentre of the Vaucluse plain which produces pink Cavaillon melons, fleshy Marmande tomatoes, violet, spiky artichokes, peaches, cherries, pears, apples and strawberries. The Vaucluse also enjoys a reputation for its early, green tipped asparagus. It's the same variety as the white speared Argenteuil asparagus, but instead of the tip being kept buried under a mound of soil until it is ready to be picked, which keeps the stem white, it is allowed to poke its head above ground and ripen in the sunlight.

British epicures always preferred the 'little gentlemen in green', a commercial fact which was not lost on the great French chef Auguste Escoffier. During a break from his duties at the Savoy during the 1890s, he went into a café at Mérindol, a village outside Cavaillon and met some of the region's asparagus growers. 'Gentlemen,' he told them, 'you produce beautiful asparagus, but it's labour intensive and doesn't reward you fairly for your efforts. I live in London where I manage the kitchens of a grand hotel. And the English prefer green asparagus. If you were interested in growing them I could guarantee you big profits.'

Apparently, the market gardeners hummed and haaed until a young man pointed out that there were always some small asparagus left in the ground after the harvest, which were worth virtually nothing. If they were allowed to grow out of the soil they would turn the desired colour. Thereafter, only green asparagus was exported to Britain and the reputation of the *asperge de Lauris* (the village next to Mérindol) was made. Rather testily, Escoffier complained in his memoires: 'I never received so much as one bunch of asparagus from a producer as a token of thanks. However, my advice certainly made the fortunes of some of them.'

Carpentras' sweets, Berlingots, have a pedigree as old as the city's association with the French Popes. The word itself is a deformation of Bertrand de Goth who became Clement V. The story goes that at a banquet held in his honour in 1313, the head patissier had prepared a dessert of candied and crystallized fruits hanging from the branches of two small trees served with liqueur-flavoured custards which were decorated with golden caramel threads. Because he had a little boiled sugar and caramel left over, he combined the two ingredients, flavoured his mixture with mint and lemon essence and pulled it out to form little candy sticks. These were served to Pope Clement on a silver salver with the instructions: 'All honour to Bertrand de Goth. To be cut up with a golden chisel.'

How a golden chisel just happened to be on hand is not clear, but his Holiness broke up the sticks and passed them around to the guests.

The latterday Berlingot is as much a humbug as any other boiled sweet. It's manufactured industrially and sold in every patisserie in pretty tins which probably cost more to make than the sweets themselves. That does not detract from their innocent charm. I bought my ration in a chocolate box of a patisserie, *Clavel*, close to the Porte d'Orange. The shop-window is shaped like a varnished mahogany frame and was filled with goodies; multicoloured truffles, almond Calissons, Berlingots, a tower made of nougatine and chocolate crazy paving. The last is infinitely preferable to barley sugar boiled Berlingots. It's no more than roughly broken slabs of variously flavoured chocolate. The old lady serving let me try most of them, until her daughter arrived and virtually shooed her out of the shop.

Clavel
RUE PORTE D'ORANGE
CARPENTRAS
TELEPHONE 90 63 07 59

Hostellerie du Roy Soleil
84560 MENERBES
TELEPHONE 90 72 51 54

Carpentras is also renowned for its *tians*; large, shallow-sided elliptical stoneware dishes, and the vegetables of all kinds that are baked in them. Sliced potatoes, mixed with garlic and bay leaf are doused with oil and left to soften and eventually brown in a low oven. Cubes of marrow, dusted with flour, are baked with parsley and garlic until the top turns to an almost charcoal crust. The Romantic poet Mistral gives a recipe for a *tian* of spinach, purslane, herbs and salt fish baked with an egg custard and *tians* of aubergines, courgettes and tomatoes combined to form a dish which was a precursor of *ratatouille*. The variety of *tian* recipes testifies to the many different vegetables grown in abundance around the town, but it does not imply that the peasants of a century ago were richer here than elsewhere in Provence. Most of them would have prepared their *tians* at home and taken them to the village baker to be cooked in his oven after he had finished with the bread.

John Hughes, on his tour of Provence early last century, admired 'a profusion

Edible art in Clavel *patisserie's window.*

of every sort of esculent vegetables which the inhabitants cultivate with great assiduity'. He attributed this to the quality of the 'pet dunghill' standing in front of every house, put there, he suggested, because the proud owner could not bear to be out of its sight.

From Carpentras I headed south to Cavaillon. It's famous for its orange-pink cantaloup melons which ripen by the ton under glass or plastic cloches from the early spring, and then in fields up to the end of summer. Alexandre Dumas *fils*, author of *La Dame aux Camelias* and in 1873 the *Grand Dictionnaire de la Cuisine* reached an agreement with the mayor of Cavaillon whereby he would supply his complete works, consisting of about 300 volumes, to the town in exchange for an annual income of a dozen locally-grown melons. As an early example of a public relations exercise, on both sides, it was a singularly well-managed coup which enhanced the reputation for good taste on both sides.

Choosing the right, ripe melon from a market stall demands vigilance and concentration. There are four classic pointers. First, the skin should be calloused and rough to the touch. The stalk which attaches to the fruit somewhat like an elongated nipple (the proper term is a 'crown') should be slightly raised. If you press on either side of the stalk at the top of the melon, there should be some give. Lastly, the melon should have a characteristic perfume. Some amateurs tap the melon to feel whether it is full and juicy or hollow and hold it in the hand to check whether it seems heavy.

Pouring cheap port over a perfectly good melon is one of the most obvious nonsenses invented by English cooks. The parma ham thing may be a good idea for those who have an unlimited access to ripe melons, but on a hot summer's day the best way to eat a Cavaillon melon is by itself. It should not require sugar. In fact, it's not a bad idea to squeeze a couple of drops of lemon juice on it. The tartness heightens the perfumed aroma.

Cavaillon is supposed to have the highest per capita income of any French town. This prosperity is due almost entirely to its being the central distribution point for the fruit and vegetables grown in the Vaucluse plain. It's not picturesque. The centre is small, a shade unkempt and dusty. Fleets of articulated trucks fill the parking lots on the outskirts. There were coaches leaving in all directions, except where I wanted to go, and the railway station only connects with Avignon. So I found myself hitching again.

By good luck the first car to stop was driven by the Ménerbes chemist who was going back to work after his midday siesta. He was a young Parisian, missing the big city, who had come south because he could not afford to set up a practice closer to home. He did not enjoy country living, and had rented a flat in Cavaillon rather than buy a property. One of the traditional tasks of the village pharmacist is to judge whether a wild mushroom is edible or not. I asked him whether many different species were brought for his inspection. He admitted that he was not an expert mycologist, but he knew the main edible varieties. He had only been asked for an opinion on a few occasions. Mostly, it was the older inhabitants who went mushroom hunting and they knew what was what.

Ménerbes is one of the spectacular hill villages dotted around the Vaucluse. Some, such as Bonnieux, Gordes or Roussillon have responded to the requirements of summer visitors by creating the necessary infrastructure of luxury hotel, restaurants, pizzerias, potteries and museums. Others such as St Saturnin d'Apt, and Ménerbes attract their ration of sightseers, but these tend not to linger.

The village's present charm relies less on the fact that it is full of quaint natives, which it isn't, than on it's having been harnessed by comfortably off, civilized romantics: bankers, lawyers and artists. I knocked on the door of a house with clear blue shutters, and pink cyclamens. It belonged to the artist, Jane Eakin.

I did not know Jane, but carried an introduction to her house-guest, Priscilla Eissen. Having apologized for arriving with little or no notice, I offered them the bottles from the Domaine des Girasols. We sat outside drinking white Côtes du Rhône on a pocket-handkerchief of a lawn overlooking the Lubéron Mountains. Late, on an autumn afternoon the landscape was imbued with the mystic quality of a Chinese painting, with terraces cut from the slopes, an isolated farmhouse perched on a knoll and misty haze separating the layers of hills from the woods which emerge from the valley.

After dark, we dined at a tiny restaurant in the village, *La Galerie*. Its owner, Micäel Reboul, had learned his craft at *L'Oustau de Beaumanière*, Raymond Thuilier's

La Galerie

MICAEL REBOUL

RUE MARCELLIN-PONCET

84560 MENERBES

TELEPHONE 90 72 31 81

luxury inn, built below the ruins of the medieval ghost town, Les Baux de Provence. Not that he was over-respectful of his Alma Mater: 'The place has gone down,' he lamented. 'It does what we call *cuisine à la pizza*. It takes a couple of hundred bookings and the food is not cooked properly.'

That may be an over-harsh criticism. Even if the cooking at *L'Oustau de Beaumanière* does not always live up to its three-star Michelin rating, just being there is a moment of special privilege, because of its wild setting. Les Baux, an outcrop of les Alpilles, a rocky bauxite chain between Arles and Avignon, was described by the writer Quentin Crewe as a 'tame panther on a silken leash, tame for only as long as it chooses to acquiesce in the game of being a pet.'

What Micäel Reboul has eloped with is an exceptional wine from a vineyard carved out of the steep, scree-covered slopes of the Alpilles. The Domaine de Trévallon is on the back-road between St Rémy-de-Provence and St Etienne-du-Grès. Its ex-architect owner, Eloi Durbach, produces a noble wine lacking an *appellation contrôlée*, because it contains a large proportion of Cabernet-Sauvignon grapes which are considered atypical of the region. But his deep, rich red wine is unique in Provence. It has a complex taste of concentrated fruit and tannins with the special advantage of costing far less than it is worth.

La Galerie's menu was short, no more than a dozen dishes, and many of them featuring a medley of seasonal wild mushrooms. They came as a garnish for a duck salad with pickled grapes, for beef and for salmon served with a light chlorophyll tinted watercress sauce. It was a carefully prepared meal, and for three of us it cost less than many sophisticated restaurants in Provence, especially those on the Côte d'Azur, charge for one person. I would willing go back to the *Galerie*, but Priscilla took a friend there a few days later and was poisoned by a wild mushroom which put her on her back for 48 hours. Either Monsieur Reboul had not checked his stock with the pharmacist or the latter was even less knowledgeable about fungi than he had admitted to being.

I spent the night at the *Hostellerie du Roy Soleil*, in the Coulon Valley below Ménerbes. As I was settling up, I asked whether the hotel made its own jams. Those on which I had breakfasted were delicious – thick fruity strawberry and apricot

The angular skyline of Ménerbes, a sophisticated village in the hills.

conserves which could be swallowed by the spoonful. The patronne gave me a hard appraising stare. No, she said, they came from the nearby town of Apt. If I was going there she would give me the address. She scribbled it on a scrap of paper.

L'Isle-sur-la-Sorgue market
Sunday

It was Sunday morning. Priscilla collected me early and we drove the few miles to L'Isle-sur-la-Sorgue to browse around the market. It's certainly one of the most picturesque markets, threading its way along the quays facing the River Sorgue and boring into the alleys of this island townlet. The antique dealers have the prime pitches close to the water, and there is room to examine anything from old corkscrews to clasp knives for pruning vines, earthenware *daubières* for cooking stews, hand-painted plates from the Provençal pottery centre of Moustiers and seventh-hand Yves Montand records. The only items in short supply are bargains.

At the end of the bric-à-brac stalls was a man selling pickles and jams. Jars were open for tasting. There was a sticky milk jam, sliced onion pickles with tarragon and a rare grape conserve, *Le Raisiné*, prepared by boiling back the pulp and juice till it forms a thick mass. On a corner of the stall lay a pile of slim volumes entitled *Confitures, Traditionnelles et Exotiques*. I bought a copy of the book, rather than any of the jam, which had been put into recycled jars and might not have survived five weeks' shaking in an already overstuffed bag.

The narrow streets were packed. At *Marchés Louis Charcuteries Salaisons* which sells dozens of salted, smoked and dried *saucissons*, we bought a selection of the more unusual ones and went to try them over coffee in the *Café de France*. Priscilla nibbled a slice of *chèvre* and commented that it tasted like a goat's bum. She was right. A *saucisson* made from donkey meat was very dark and gamey like biltong (dried antelope meat), even more so than a boar sausage which was leaner and similar to ordinary *saucisson sec*. Our best finds were a *chapelet aux noix* and a *chapelet aux noisettes*, small *saucissons* sold in links, which contain pieces of walnut or hazelnut.

We met Jane in the café and with her another Ménerbes artist, Joe Downey. He was sceptical of the milk jam in the market: 'It's the same as the condensed milk which we used to eat with a spoon as children.' Years spent in Ménerbes had thickened his skin against putative regional specialities, but he mentioned with affection his local baker who made authentic madeleines. These scalloped cakes taken with a cup of tea were the spark which ignited Marcel Proust's imagination and started him composing his epic memoire *A La Recherche Du Temps Perdu.*

We went to lunch in a packed, serious little restaurant at Cabrières d'Avignon a few miles outside L'Isle-sur-la-Sorgue. *Le Bistrot à Michel*, in complete contrast with the antique furniture and Kashmir wall hangings of *La Galerie*, had cramped tables, theatrical posters stuck at random and variously priced menus, ranging from soup, meat and pud to *foie gras*. Madame Bosc, a dark-eyed welterweight in black slacks who once worked as a waitress in Glasgow, danced round the room scattering plates with absolute professionalism. She greeted Priscilla not as an old friend, but as a regular client who required a mild reproach for arriving a few minutes late.

The soup, ordered from the cheapest menu, was a thin tasteless broth which promised the worst, but a main course *porcelet*, which I suppose should be translated as an outsize sucking pig, was faultless; the meat tender, the sauce thickened with blood and faintly flavoured with fennel as black and glossy as Japanese lacquer. A bottle of *Château Canorgue* from the Lubéron left me feeling like André Gide who knew 'The heavy wine of inns which comes back with a taste of violet and procures the thick sleep of midday.'

Le Bistrot à Michel
CABRIERES-D'AVIGNON
TELEPHONE 90 76 82 08

4

KITCHENS IN THE HILLS

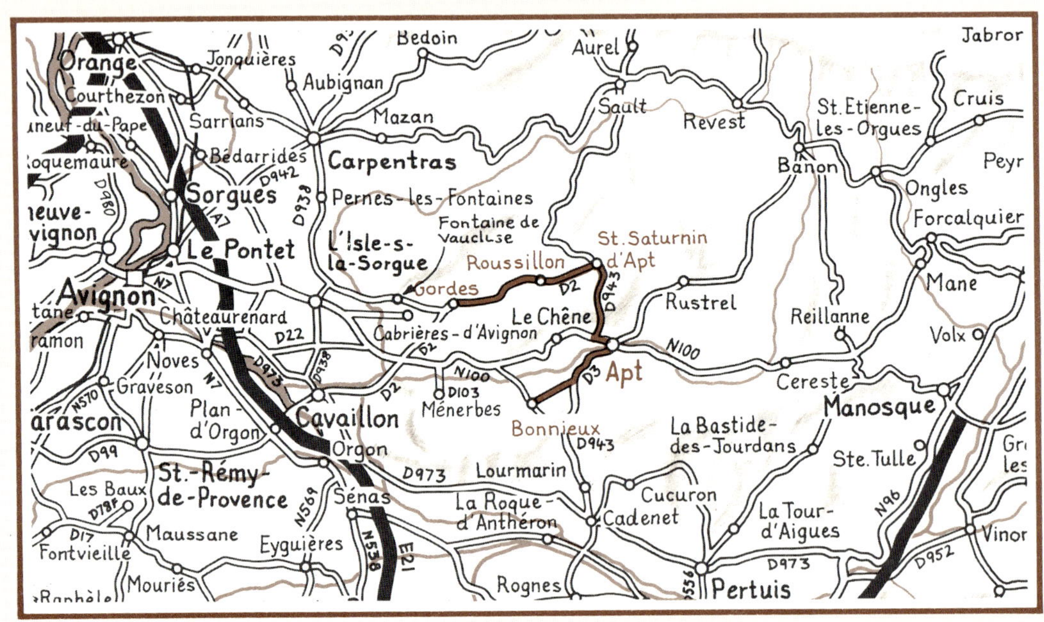

Bonnieux – Apt – St Saturnin d'Apt – Roussillon – Gordes

As Joe Downey had offered to leave me a few madeleines in his letterbox, Priscilla drove back to Ménerbes to collect them. The grooved cakes are made to a classic 'quatre-quarts' recipe from equal quantities of sugar, eggs, flour and butter. These had obviously been hand-made because the crumb had little air pockets – flaws which would never suit a manufacturer – and they tasted of real eggs and butter.

Like many of the hilltop villages in the Vaucluse, Ménerbes has tentacles of narrow roads curling out in all directions. I wanted to go to Bonnieux about five miles distant to visit the bread museum there. The road passes Lacoste where the Marquis de Sade lived before he was 'embastilled' as the Michelin *Guide Vert* so neatly expresses it.

Bonnieux's museum, in a converted bakery, preserves as relics tools which the bakers at Sarrians still use on a daily basis. It traces breadmaking history in France from Gallo-Roman times when the dough was leavened with beer, to the Revolution when the loaves had to be made, by law, to a standard recipe of three parts wheat to one part rye.

Monsieur Valette, the curator, explained that in the past *fougasses*, the savoury breads I had seen in Sarrians and which are considered to be typical Provençal fare used to be the dough trimmings which were put into the oven to test whether it was hot enough. Flavouring these edible 'off-cuts' with bits of anchovies or olives was never done systematically. The *fougasses aux grattelons*, made with little scraps of fried salt pork or bacon were as common, if not even more so, in the South West and around Bordeaux.

Recipes which are now household names have probably evolved from the same left-over source. *Quiche Lorraine*, until modern cooks adopted it, was based on a bread dough. The pizza with its tomato topping is an Italian cousin of the *fougasse*. So is *pissaladière*, the Niçois onion tart. Larger towns on the Riviera now produce *fougasses* in factories for sale as French fast food. Elitists might well turn up their noses at these cloned copies of the rustic real thing, but they do at least provide an alternative to the sterile fast food *à l'Americaine* which sometimes seems to be swamping the high streets and town centres.

Musée de la Boulangerie

RUE DE LA REPUBLIQUE

84480 BONNIEUX

TELEPHONE 90 75 88 34

A reliable confiserie in Apt:

Marcel Richaud

ANGLE QUAI DE LA LIBERTE

APT

TELEPHONE 90 74 43 50

Growing cereals as a staple crop has long ceased to be an essential part of Provençal agriculture. A few ruined windmills on deserted hilltops are the only evidence that wheat ever grew. The strain which was planted, La Tuzelle, might have become extinct had not a team of agricultural detectives traced it to a farm where it was being fed to chickens.

Although the local *Syndicat d'Initiative*, the tourist bureau-cum-gossip-shop of French village communities, did its best to find me a bed, all rooms in Bonnieux were taken. It was the weekend of All Saints, they explained, a national holiday. The nearest town was Apt, so I took a taxi there. I asked the driver to take me to a reasonable hotel and she found me a comfortable inn close to the River Calavon which flows through the town centre.

Apt has an ambivalent reputation for its jams and glacé fruits. Many of the gaudy, sticky cherries which finish up in crumbly English fruit cakes started life here. Surprisingly enough, they were once genuine fruit, though every hint of flavour is extracted from them to be replaced with sugar syrup. The coal-tar dye, Erythrosine, supplies their synthetic rouge.

Long before the town became associated with the unreal cherry, its artisans had learnt how to candy melons, peaches, plums, figs, citrus fruits and angelica. A handful of them still survive. The owners of these small independent confiseries used to keep crocks into which they dropped all the left-over pieces of sugar drenched fruit and syrup. Dollops of this mish-mash confectionery were spooned out to children and went by the name of Apt Jam.

Like the *cachat*, sold in the cheese shop at Vaison-La-Romaine, it was a process devised to prevent waste, not a special recipe. An Aptesten cautionary tale tells of an inquisitive child who always asked his mother what this or that shapeless lump in the jam was. She would reply: 'That's a little mouse, my child. Now eat it up, dear.' It became a routine game and the mother used to say the same thing without bothering to look. One day the child dipped into the crock and extracted a real mouse which had fallen in and drowned in the syrup. 'Is that a mouse too?' asked the child. The story has an open ending.

The scrap of paper given me in Ménerbes at the *Hostellerie du Roy Soleil* bore the address, 35 Impasse de la Chastelle. It supplied no clue as to what kind of a jam-smith I might expect. At the back of my mind was the picture of some grey-haired granny figure. Finding the place took a while: it was at the far end of a seedy row of terraced houses off the main Cavaillon road. The man who opened the front door recognized me before I could make up my mind where exactly I had seen him before. He was one of the traders who had been selling preserves on the market at L'Isle-sur-la-Sorgue.

His partner, older and bearded, was hunched at a kitchen table, drinking rosé from a tumbler, and rolling a cigarette. In front of him were a couple of copper basins filled with freshly shredded onions and beside them a knife. At the back of the room, fastened to a slatted bamboo screen covering some dull wallpaper, was a blackboard with a string of thin, red, drying chillies hanging from it. In large, awkward capitals, one of the men had written 'HYPERSOMNIE' and below it in smaller letters a string of figures from a recipe. Pasted next to the board was a torn sticker stating: 'Chase away the Natural and it comes galloping back.'

It was not easy to connect this cold, almost oppressive room and the melancholic man with the cherry and hibiscus, the peach and bergamot tea jams, or the deep golden apricot preserve with its chunks of fruit that I'd seen on the market. I sat down, accepted a glass of wine and told them how I had spent the previous evening reading the book they had sold me. The younger man, who had attacked another onion nodded toward his partner and said: 'He wrote it.'

Jean-Yves Cannepin used to be a chef. He said he had worked in Brazil and Chile, had owned a chic restaurant in Brussels and then a bistro on Ibeza. 'I'm forty-nine,' he explained. 'Nobody would employ me now.' There was no trace of bitterness, just a recognition that he could no longer stand the pace of a professional kitchen. He had returned to live in his native Apt where as a child he had watched his mother, grandmother and aunts making preserves. Cooking was the only skill he had (he had no money), so he decided to apply it, and make a living by following a traditional Aptesten craft.

He and Robert had started the business with just the two pans and a single gas burner, and they were not planning to expand at all. They weighed their ingredients on an antique set of scales with a back-to-front dial which was read from a mirror set at an angle to it. He had bought it off an antique dealer in the market at L'Isle-sur-la-Sorgue.

To judge the setting point of the jams they relied on trial and error, testing the consistency with the back of a spoon. They never bothered with a thermometer. Nor did they sterilize the jars or warm them before pouring in the boiling sugar. Modern pots do not crack, he claimed.

They always worked as I had seen them doing, sitting around a kitchen table, usually with a glass of wine and maybe a cigarette. The man from the *Services Vétérinaires*, a body responsible for public hygiene, had paid them a visit and given them a clean bill of health. Jean-Yves opened a cupboard and showed me a jar in a box stamped with a seal. The official had taken away three jams, ostensibly to test, but only one was returned. The others had been eaten in the interest of science and public health.

Robert who had gone to buy fruit at the local wholesale market returned with an armful of gingerines. He had bought seventy kilos of them, and there was a sharp exchange between the men as to whether their cash-flow would stand the outlay.

The gingerine is used exclusively for jam in the Lubéron. It looks like an outsize marrow, but it's closer to a water melon, and can weigh upwards of five kilos. After scooping out the seeds, the flesh is cut into strips, macerated in sugar and boiled with orange and lemon slices together with a vanilla pod for extra flavour. When they have finished cooking, the gingerine pieces have turned transparent.

In summer, Robert and Jean-Yves could sell whatever they produced. They did well in the tourist villages like Gordes, but in winter, it was a struggle. Because they never cut corners and only bought the best fruit they could find, they charged more than the supermarkets. Whatever the time of year, they lived hand to mouth and when they did not feel like doing anything, they took the day off.

Jean-Yves' *Confitures Traditionnelles et Exotiques* is a treasure-trove of a cookery book, because it contains some of the most fanciful, imaginative concoctions anyone could ever hope to discover. Yet underpinning them is a respect for the old ways as well as a mastery of technique.

Bonnieux houses an extraordinary museum devoted to the history of bread.

Le Platane
ODILE BORDES
PLACE JULES FERRY
APT
TELEPHONE 90 74 14 17

It's the work of someone totally at ease with fruit. He describes how to make a jam with early purple figs, flavouring them with red Lubéron wine and cinnamon. Another jam uses the September figs with brown sugar and vanilla. His advice for mango jam is that it is easier to make in the Congo, and that there is a variety of green mango which should be avoided because it tastes of turpentine. He cooks chestnut preserve and flavours it with mocha; he mixes hazelnuts with lemon and lime, *bigarreaux* cherries with fennel and Montmorency cherries with beer. He folds honey into a traditional carrot jam.

Did he really test all these recipes and did they work? 'Well,' he admitted, 'the last recipe in the book for a tricolour jelly is a bit difficult to get right, because the colours keep running into each other.'

Odile Bordes liked Jean-Yves: 'He comes here for warmth.' She runs her bistro *Le Platane* on a shoe-string, so she had something in common with the jamsmith, but her energy was in direct contrast to his lassitude. She had left a career in linguistics to open a restaurant, fulfilling a ten-year ambition. She was self-taught or rather self-teaching, acquiring the skills of her profession as she went along. She volunteered that she had seen Jean-Yves at work and felt herself a novice in comparison.

She does all the cooking herself from a galley tucked to one side of a dining-room decorated with high-contrast photographs of a rock group on tour. What did the 10,000 stolid provincial citizens make of an atmosphere which would have seemed cool in the Latin Quarter? 'I have two clienteles. The elderly come at seven and we play them Vivaldi or Mozart. After nine it's jazz.' The food and wine is the same for both groups.

It costs about 100 francs to eat honourably at *Le Platane*. Odile does what she can to keep down prices: she goes directly to the producers to buy wine in bulk and bottles it herself. She can't afford expensive raw materials. She certainly does not have the means to buy large quantities of truffles – despite the fact that Apt has the biggest professional truffle market in the Vaucluse.

'Knowing about very good produce and being able to buy it are two different things.' Lamb produced in the Lubéron is renowned. It has its own *appellation contrôlée*, *Agneau Soleil*, which guarantees that it has been bred and reared within the boundaries of the Lubéron Regional Park. It's in fierce competition with the Sisteron lamb reared on the slopes of the Durance Valley at the northern edge of Provence and the lamb reared on the Alpilles.

The Lubéron farmers have to contend with rustlers. One woman's herd of the rare, horned chèvres du Rove had been stolen by a goat thief: it was months before he was caught in one of the wilder corners of the park. Combing 100,000 hectares to trace the goats could not have been an easy task for the police.

Odile bought the cheaper cuts of Lubéron lamb to make her speciality, a *terrine d'agneau*. The meat was marinated in Banyuls, a fortified wine, minced with duck fat and baked in a *bain-marie*. It had a clean taste of the meat, slightly sweet, and a texture rather more firm than a pâté made from pork. She served it with small gherkins and onions, but felt that it would taste better by itself.

Nearly all the Provençal cookery books I've ever read suggest sticking the legs of lamb with slivers of garlic and/or anchovy before roasting them. This is fair enough for the older lambs, young mutton really, which have spent months grazing on the hillsides and developing firm red muscle. But the finest lamb, the spring lamb which was once served as part of the traditional Easter feast, has meat which is almost white, like veal, and has the faintest pink juice. To spike it with anything at all would be a heresy.

I left *Le Platane* in three minds. I could go to Saignon on the Castellet road to see a friend of Odile's who grew ancient tomato varieties. Jean-Yves had advised me to visit the Colorado de Rustrel north-east of Apt, gigantic quarries supplying the ochre which contributes so much to the colour of Provence. A third option was to investigate a new high performance duck, the FN3, being bred on a poultry farm.

Instead, I hitched a ride with a hunter in a *deux chevaux*, who was going to shoot thrushes in the hills around St Saturnin d'Apt. He recommended the restaurant *St Hubert* to me as having good game dishes on its menu, especially a terrine of unspecified birds, namely thrushes. It was closed. Having booked in at the *Hôtel-Restaurant des Voyageurs*, a simple stop-over *pension* for ramblers on hiking holidays on the rocky Plateau de Vaucluse, I wandered up through the hillside village into the castle dominating it.

Hôtel-Restaurant des Voyageurs

84490 ST SATURNIN D'APT

TELEPHONE 90 75 42 08

The ruins stretched along a narrow ridge with a vertiginous drop on either side towards a small chapel. Already, the *garrigue* has started to reassert its authority over the broken stone walls. Savory's powerful aroma dominated the more subtle scents of thyme and marjoram. Stumpy juniper bushes with berries clinging between the spiny leaves were struggling to put down roots in any spare cranny. Even after sunset, when the silhouettes of the Lubéron hills beyond Apt stood out like pyramids, the repetitive pop, pop of shotguns peppered the air.

Game is becoming so scarce in these parts that hunters outnumber the hunted. Quail comes from farms now. So does pheasant. A few genuine wild boar skulk in the wooded coverts which have escaped the ravages of forest fires, but most have been bred in captivity and crossed with pigs. On a good day the hunters in the Vaucluse may bag a red partridge. Rabbits are plentiful, but hares have become an endangered species, although a few still roam the regional parks and Mont Ventoux. René Jouveau, author of *La Cuisine Provençale de Tradition Populaire*, points out that Provençal hares are shorter in the body than those imported from outside the region. Game merchants apparently disguise the fact by trussing an imposter and leaving it to chill overnight, after which it is impossible to distinguish the foreigner from a 'Good old Ventoux hare'. Woodcock and snipe migrate across Provence, but in diminishing numbers. Wild duck are localized around the Camargue. That leaves four or five varieties of thrush; shooting them is frowned upon by the authorities, but still goes on unchecked.

Back at the *Hôtel-Restaurant des Voyageurs* a couple of hikers had collared the innkeeper's wife. On their afternoon walk, they had picked a bag of mushrooms. Would the chef mind cooking them for dinner? She disappeared into the kitchen with their catch and returned without it, so presumably they were in luck. The hotel's dining-room was adorned with photos, water-colours and a model *borie*, the stone hut, shaped like a beehive, which shelters shepherds on the exposed hillsides and in some villages used to serve as a home.

Hare terrine was on the menu. It was garnished with olives, radishes and accompanied by a bottle of Château de l'Isolette, a good wine produced near Bonnieux. Not knowing the hare's origins didn't stop me enjoying it.

St Saturnin d'Apt, where wild herbs grow among broken walls.

Fressure, the main dish, was an offal-lover's delight – a stew of lamb's liver, kidney, heart, lung and tripe in a sharp, peppery sauce flavoured with plenty of herbs and red wine. Afterwards came a fresh goat's cheese, sour and grassy, tasting like old-fashioned cottage cheese, which was left to stand until it curdled. The bill was a trifling 85 francs. It was not refined cooking by any stretch of the imagination, but it was honest and homely.

Foreign travellers who enjoy little dinners like this wonder why they cannot find the same quality at the same price in their own country. There are several reasons. In the provinces, most restaurant customers eat from the set menu, so there is little waste and the right quantity of food is bought in each day. Because the businesses are family owned and run – the patronne served over two dozen customers by herself – the wage bill is low. The family has often owned the property for several generations, so there is no mortgage. If the food costs are high, the wines are cheap to buy, and it's commonplace in French restaurants to multiply the bought-in price by three or four to achieve a healthy profit for the patron.

Offal has always been popular in Provence. It has a key part in one very grisly folk story, set in Roussillon, the next village to St Saturnin d'Apt. Raymond, the local *seigneur*, had a wife, Marguerite, who enjoyed the company of Guillaume de Cabestaing, one of his young retainers. Raymond became jealous, lured the youth out of the castle, killed him, chopped off his head and cut out his heart. He gave the heart to the cook as a piece of venison and 'enjoined him to cook it with an appropriate seasoning'. The heart was served up to Marguerite.

'Do you know what kind of meat you have been tucking into?' Seigneur Raymond asked.

'I haven't a clue,' his wife replied, 'but it was exquisite.'

'I can believe that, since it belonged to something you cherished and it is fitting that you should love dead what you did living.'

'What do you mean?'

Raymond showed her Guillaume's bloody head. 'Here is the one whose heart you have just eaten.'

'Ah, yes,' said the lady, 'I found this morsel which your barbarity has fed me so delicious that I shall never taste another for fear that I should forget its flavour. You have done me a service by giving me what belonged to me by right.'

The *seigneur* flew into a rage and rushed to stab her, but Marguerite threw herself out of the window onto the rocks.

Next morning I passed Roussillon on my way to Gordes. Raymond's castle has been flattened, but the village – ochre houses fastened to red, carmine, rosy and golden-tinted ochre cliffs – is an ideal setting for the gory yarn.

I would have enjoyed exploring its narrow streets, but had arranged to meet the patronne of a brand-new, very chic restaurant. Elisabeth Bourgeois-Baique opened her first restaurant, *Le Petit Bedon* in Avignon, in 1972. She sold up, ran the kitchens of a smart hotel outside Aix-en-Provence, married, bought a run-down farmhouse at Les Imberts, a hamlet on the fringes of Gordes and from it created *Le Mas Tourteron.*

Gordes is a very smart village, an inland St Tropez. It has its share of rich retirement homes and *résidences secondaires* for those who can afford to fly down from Paris for the weekend. In summer, it fills with hungry visitors in search of a taste of Provence. That may make it a perfect spot to launch a sophisticated restaurant, but Elisabeth Bourgeois still has to struggle for recognition. The gastronomic restaurant in France is a male dominated profession. Bodies such as the Association of Master Chefs and the *Société des Cuisiniers* exclude women, and few first-class kitchens employ young female staff, which increases the difficulty of learning the craft. Paul Bocuse, an unrepentant phallocrat, whose worldwide reputation over two decades made him the uncrowned emperor of French Master Chefs, accused women cooks of lacking imagination. He argued that it was illegal for a woman to wear the white toque symbol of the chef's authority. It's fine, he implied, for the fair sex to stay home and cook for their families, or even run a cosy bistro, but such dabblings should not pass for Culinary Art.

His criticism galvanized a handful of women chefs to found its own body, the *Association Internationale de Restauratrices Cuisinières*, of which Madame Bourgeois is a member. Setting aside its claims – 'Women cook with more feeling than men'; 'Women are the true protectors of traditional regional cuisine', both of which

Le Mas Tourteron

ELISABETH BOURGEOIS
CHEMIN ST BLAISE
LES IMBERTS GORDES
TELEPHONE 90 68 11 79

Association Internationale de Restauratrices (ARC) Cuisinières

11 RUE BARBET-DE-JOUY
75007 PARIS
TELEPHONE 45 55 15 29

An inland St Tropez, Gordes attracts many well-off weekenders.

Elisabeth Bourgeois runs a rare, and superb, all-female kitchen.

statements have more than a grain of truth – the ARC has provided a soft cushion against a real sense of isolation which female cooks experience.

That said, the kitchen at *Le Mas Tourteron* operated as no male kitchen that I've ever seen. It was spotless, and stayed that way throughout the service. And it was silent. The orders were brought to the kitchen and read out, not bawled by some *aboyeur*, the 'barker' of classical brigades. Evelyne and Armel, Madame's two cooks, dressed in whites, with sweatbands over their brows, worked quietly and never crashed and clattered the pans on the stove as an aggressive commis chef of 20 would instinctively do.

When the customers start to arrive, Madame greets them, sometimes inviting them into the kitchen, which is open to public scrutiny through a pair of double doors leading out of the bar, sometimes ushering them into the dining-room. Her girls work on either side of a black, Molténi range, the Rolls-Royce of French ovens. At first, a single pan of veal stock simmers on it, but new pots and *sauteuses* quickly join it, emitting aromas of shellfish, white wine, butter and of meat sizzling in the pan as it forms a brown, caramelized crust.

Miniature *brochettes* are grilled on cocktail sticks. Fillets of tiny red mullet are seized for a few seconds on the flesh side only and set aside. Chicken livers are sautéed until a pearl of blood rises to the surface and they are ready to be assembled for a *tarte sablée de foies blonds et poireaux nouveaux*, a fine tartlet filled with baby leeks and chicken livers. Lamb charlottes steam in a *bain-marie*. It's a favourite dish with many customers. Leg of lamb is half-roasted with thyme and garlic, then sliced and put into a mould lined with aubergines, between layers of sliced tomato, garlic and more aubergines.

There are seven pans on the top when Madame comes into the kitchen to help. She slips off her sling-backs and aims a stockinged foot at the cat. Plates leave the kitchen bearing *pétales de morue fraîche en aïoli*, flaked salt cod with a garlic mayonnaise or *filet de dorade en écailles et sa crème bachique*, filleted bream simmered in white Côtes du Rhône.

By now the number of pans in use has risen to 14. Madame crosses the kitchen to where one of the girls is garnishing a plate with beans. 'Merde!' she shouts. The girl wilts: she has run out of mushrooms and supplied an alternative garnish for an *émincé de boeuf*, sliced fillet of beef. It's not professional. The customer will be displeased. No recriminations follow. The point is made.

For dessert nearly all the customers are ordering a hot chocolate *tarte*. It's more of a cake really: a dozen eggs, a pound of melted butter, a pound of chocolate and a couple of scoops each of sugar and flour, combined to a dropping consistency. The trick is in the precise cooking. The mixture is poured into tins to a depth of an inch and baked in an oven which combines steam and dry heat at 103°C. The '*tartes*', extra moist and melting, are served with pots of hot chocolate sauce. And the cooking still goes on. Tiny almond sponges, like baby madeleines have to be baked and served warm as *petits fours*.

At the end of service Madame returns to the dining-room to speak to her departing guests. Not so much as a drip of sauce has spilled onto the flounces of her white uniform. By four, the last of the diners has gone and she can grab some lunch. That is unusual too. In most restaurants, the team of chefs sits down to eat before service starts. Afterwards Madame will relax for an hour or so before she, Evelyne, Armel and Florence in the dining-room prepare for the evening's work.

5

OF POPES AND CROCODILES

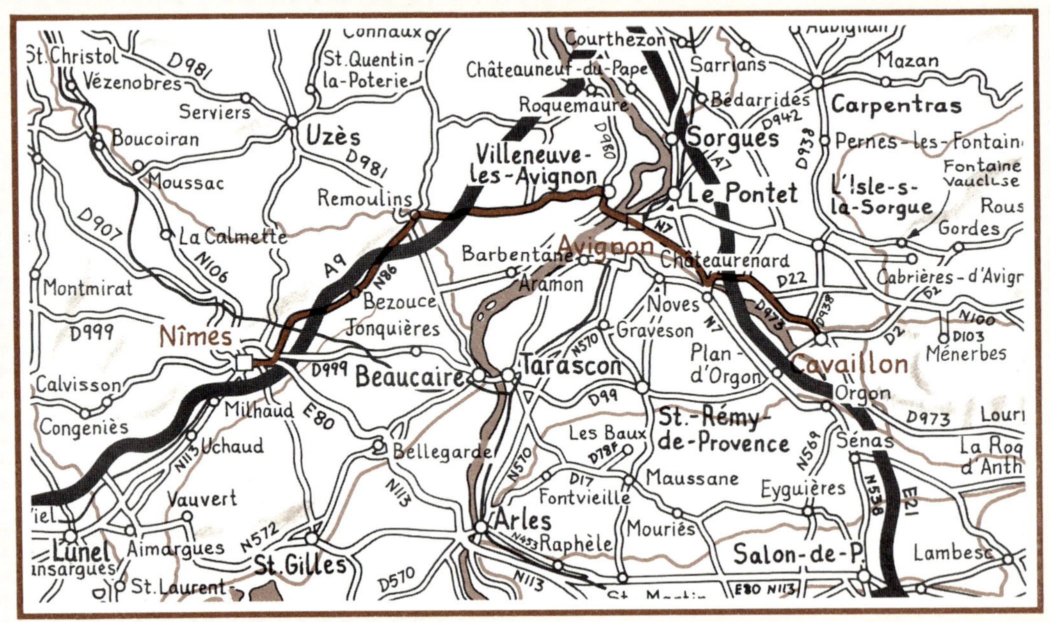

Cavaillon – Avignon – Nîmes

The hotel Elisabeth recommended was *La Ferme de la Huppe*, 'Hoopoe's Farm', a converted 18th-century, stone *mas* with six bedrooms, run by a Swiss mother-and-son team. My half-timbered room looked out on a grassy courtyard with a well, an olive tree and a large black griffon keeping guard. I'd spent several nights sleeping in village inns and above cafés, and it was soothing to discover somewhere with the comfort and informality of a well-run English country-house hotel, down to the Laura Ashley teacups at breakfast, and restrained, efficient, Swiss hospitality.

Elisabeth had promised to collect me next morning and take me to Cavaillon. While I was waiting, I dipped into a book of Lubéron cookery lying in the hotel reception. In it, Yvan Andouard, who wrote the preface, described how he would watch his aunt cooking as a boy and pester her for recipes. His Aunt Josephine had one measurement: '*un peu*', a little.

'How much oil do you put in?' he'd ask.

'A little.'

Depending on the case, it was either a little 'little', a fair 'little' or in extreme cases it could amount to a large 'little'. Anyone who aspires to mastering the art of Provençal cooking needs to solve the mystery of Aunt Josephine's 'peu'.

Cavaillon is only a quarter of an hour from Gordes, and Elisabeth dropped me at the station on her way to the central market where she did her shopping for *Le Mas Tourteron*. Trains from here to Avignon, only 25 kilometres away, are irregular and the line does a right-angle jink through L'Isle-sur-la-Sorgue, so I caught a bus which took me there more quickly. As it passed through the outer ring of industrial zones, commercial centres, hypermarkets and the airport on the fringes of the city, the walls of the medieval Palais des Papes loomed ever larger and more impressive above the outlying suburbs.

Avignon is or rather was the City of Popes – and anti-popes. Its heyday lasted through the 14th century when a succession of French pontiffs deserted Rome to live there. Clement V started the fashion. He achieved fame by outlawing the Knights Templars to the great satisfaction of Philippe Le Bel. He was noted for his taste in boiled sweets.

La Ferme de la Huppe

M. KONINGS
ROUTE D156
LES POURQUIERS
84220 GORDES
TELEPHONE 90 72 12 25

Hiély-Lucullus
5 RUE DE LA REPUBLIQUE
84000 AVIGNON
TELEPHONE 90 86 17 07

M. Hiély also owns a bistro:

La Fourchette
7 RUE RACINE
84000 AVIGNON
TELEPHONE 90 82 56 01

Another Clement, the Sixth, who built an extension of the Papal Palace which still dominates the city, earned a footnote in the history of pontifical protocol when he modified the menu served to cardinals when they were called to elect a new pope. An earlier papal bull had stipulated that they should be fed twice a day, and a single dish at each sitting, if they failed to come up with a man for the job within three days. Clement relaxed the rules by allowing the one dish to be accompanied by soup, salad, cheese, jam and fruit, ostensibly to prevent scurvy. However, he left intact the ultimate coercion, a diet of dried bread for the cardinals if they had not picked a Holy Father within eight days of sitting.

About 20 years ago, on my first visit to Avignon, I was sleeping in the cheapest hotel money could buy and eating in a dive off the Place St Pierre, a cobbled square behind the Palais des Papes, where the menu was an accessible 3F50. Every day, I would go on a pilgrimage around the corner into the Rue de la République, the main shopping street which bisects the centre of the city to read the menu outside *Hiély-Lucullus*. At the time it was 35F and represented the best value of any two-star Michelin restaurant in France. The trouble was that the price was exactly ten times what my dinner was costing me.

Pierre Hiély's restaurant, despite its influx of seasoned and seasonal gastronomic pilgrims, is very much a local institution, supplying cuisine of the Avignonnais bourgeois, by the bourgeois, for the bourgeois. It's located on the first floor, above a shoe-shop, and the most expensive menu still costs less than a fairly mediocre pair of loafers.

At 12.45 on a sunny weekday afternoon, I hesitated at the bottom of the stairs, much as the young man had – not because of the price of the meal, but because someone dressed like a superannuated student, humping a shoulder-bag with a broken strap does not expect a friendly reception from a bourgeois *maître d'hôtel*, especially if he does not have a reservation.

It was a very English fear, born of living in a country where, in a few choice establishments, 'gentlemen' are still expected to wear ties. I should have known better. Waiting at table is a respected profession in France, requiring tact, charm, diplomacy as well as technical skill with a corkscrew or a spoon and fork.

If there were a patron saint of head waiters he would be Vatel, the 'Great Vatel' as Madame de Sévigné refers to him, the *maître d'hôtel* of the Prince de Condé. In a letter written to her daughter at Grignan in 1671 she wrote: 'This man whose ability was distinguished above all others, whose brilliant mind was capable of supporting the cares of a State; this man whom I knew, at eight o'clock this morning, finding that his fish order had not been delivered, was unable to bear the loss of face and stabbed himself to death.'

Service at *Hiély-Lucullus*, in a classic dining-room which has never sniffed the attentions of an interior designer, has no truck with ostentation. Waitresses, none of them more than a size ten, nip between tables like ferrets down a rabbit hole. They handle customers with the aplomb of well-trained nannies, and they know their way through a warren of over 30 Châteauneuf du Papes from different vintages and from the better vineyards.

Châteauneuf du Pape, 'the pope's wine', has the second largest *appelation contrôlée* area in France (the largest is St Emilion in Bordeaux). Thirteen grape varieties are permitted in its vinification, but the character of the wine has more to do with the type of land on which the vineyards are set. The soil is covered in a layer of large, smooth pebbles, deposited by the Rhône. In July and August, when the grapes are ripening, the sun burns down on these stones which transmit their reflected heat upwards warming the shaded underbellies of the purple bunches. The result, at its best, is a powerful, purple wine which keeps for ten or even 20 years.

Frédéric Mistral admitted that this wine was one of the prime inspirations of the revival of Provençal poetry. 'It is there,' he wrote, 'in Châteauneuf, drenched by sunlight under aromatic hills, where in summer crickets creak on every side, where in autumn the glorious papal wine is pressed, that we came, twenty years old, budding poets, to make ourselves drunk on Provence.'

Not all Châteauneuf du Pape is of the same quality and some of it is rumoured to be *trafiqué*, in other words adulterated. There must be over a hundred producers, but *Le Vieux Télégraphe* (*Hiély-Lucullus* has about ten different vintages), *Clos des Papes*, *Château de Beaucastel*, *Château Rayas*, *Domaine du Père Caboche* and *Domaine de Terre Ferme* are outstanding. Another prettily named wine *Chante Cigale*, Cricket's

Châteauneuf du Pape

Names to watch out for:

Le Vieux Télégraphe
Clos des Papes
Château de Beaucastel
Château Rayas
Domaine du Père Caboche
Domaine de Terre Ferme
Chante Cigale

Song, almost matches these. The better domaine-bottled wines from the region are entitled to bear a pope's mitre embossed on the bottle. Since not all of us are expert, this is a useful indication of quality when confronted with an unfamiliar name.

The greater part of the region's production is given over to red wines – the grapes do not easily achieve the right acidity for white. But the best of the whites fetch a premium and demand for them outstrips supply. One of the Avignon Popes, Innocent VI, who was especially partial to it, drank white wine when celebrating morning mass because he found the red too hard.

The house white, served in a carafe at *Hiély-Lucullus*, is a *Château Simiane*; listed as Côtes du Rhône, it had the body, concentration and length of the equivalent Châteauneuf du Pape wines. Drunk with anchovy *sacristains* (pastry twists), as an aperitif, or with an unctuous *brandade* of salt cod, it may not have had the class of a Condrieu or white Hermitage, but it was far better than this dusty traveller had expected from a *vin du patron*.

Salted anchovies, used as a flavouring, are as old as Mediterranean history itself. Before the canning industry took over, they were prepared on a domestic scale and *La Cuisinière Provençale*, a cookery book written at the turn of the century, has a recipe which suggests colouring the salt with ochre to improve the fillets' appearance. *Anchoïade*, a cold dipping sauce made by stewing the fillets with oil and sometimes vinegar until they have reduced to a purée, is probably the most widespread use of tinned anchovies. Better still, if you can find fresh anchovies – and it's a big if, since the traditional season only lasts from 15th April until June – fillet them, salt them for half an hour or so, and eat them raw with olive-oil and bread. The Rhône, in its northern reaches towards Lyon, spawned a curious dish, *grillade de boeuf à la marinière*, which is a stew, not a grill, in which the sauce is flavoured with pounded anchovies.

Brandade de morue is more intimately associated with Avignon's neighbour, Nîmes. It's a velvety emulsion of fish, olive-oil and maybe a little milk, which has been rubbed and squeezed and pounded and turned in a mortar or beaten until the arms ache. Having said that, it would not surprise me if a food processor could do the business in a few minutes. At *Hiély-Lucullus*, this marvel is spooned into a puff-pastry coffin which melts to a thousand buttery flakes in harmony with its charge.

The Papal Palace dominates the city of Avignon.

The saddle of rabbit, roasted with its liver with a *poivrade* sauce, has been a speciality in the restaurant for many years. It's the domestic, not the wild variety of rabbit, and the care taken in its rearing for the table is every bit as conscientious as the husbandry required for, say, a Bresse chicken or a Rouennais duck. The first stage of Paul Bocuse's instructions on how to prepare a *terrine de lapin* begins: 'You have a five to six month old rabbit; in its final fortnight you feed it only oats, thyme, bran, bread and, to drink, a little milk each day. This diet fattens and perfumes it; the flesh is also very white.'

Pierre Hiély's rabbit is just what you might expect from a preparation of this kind; white-fleshed, still moist and lightly flavoured with *farigoule* (wild thyme), the liver faintly pink, the wine sauce, not quite red, not quite brown, intensely flavoured, but not harsh. Washed down with young, purple Châteauneuf du Pape, it was everything which bourgeois cooking at its best should be.

The desserts contributed to the restaurant's reputation. Bread pudding with fresh raspberry sauce and *crème anglaise* and *oeufs à la neige* – poached meringues (a convenient way for chefs to dispose of surplus egg whites), might seem ordinary in the context of earning accolades. But the fact that *Hiély* has survived the ravages of nouvelle cuisine with the brilliant, inventive, often precocious chefs thrown up by that fashion and retained its reputation and stature is proof of quality as well as its staying power.

Brunel
46 RUE DE LA BALANCE
84000 AVIGNON
TELEPHONE 90 85 24 83

L'Ermitage Meissonnier
ROUTE DE NIMES
BELLEVUE-LES-ANGLES
TELEPHONE 90 25 41 68

Avignon does have other restaurants to rival *Hiély*. Odile Bordes (from *Le Platane* in Apt) worked for a while at *Brunel*, near the Palais des Papes and thinks that the cooking there is more skilful. And *L'Ermitage Meissonier*, at Bellevue-les-Angles, a suburb of Avignon, just across the Rhône on the road to Nîmes, may be more refined and inventive. Paul-Louis Meissonier works wonders there with crayfish, truffled raviolis and little cushions of milk-fed lamb flavoured with rosemary.

But a restaurant is more than just cuisine, as the *Guide Michelin* has always recognized, and more than the sum of its parts. *Hiély-Lucullus* has kept its provincial atmosphere and yet managed to turn itself into something of an institution like such world-famous restaurants as *Lasserre* or the *Tour d'Argent* in Paris.

Sitting at the table next to me was a proper middle-aged father with a bolshie, bad-tempered son, maybe 16 years old and looking, if anything, scruffier than me. Rather than fight the aggressive offspring, papa just let the subtle food and a carefully decanted *Hermitage* do the work for him. The youth cooled, then softened and finally glowed. The rebel became a *petit-bourgeois*. It was an object lesson of gastronomy being successfully used as a means of political manipulation.

How different from the Avignon bread riots in 1539! The poor women of the town mutinied against the pope's representative, because the price of poor quality grain had grown too expensive for them to afford, whereas the best grain was being exported for profit. They raided the tithe barns and took away as much wheat as they could carry. The government brought in troops, hanged the ringleaders, had others thrashed, and burnt down the homes of all who had fled to safety. Then they recovered the wheat which had been 'stolen'.

At the height of its influence in the Middle Ages, Avignon counted 80,000 inhabitants. Plague and cholera made inroads into that number, but the city was never less than important. By contrast, the city of Nîmes, less than 40 km away, was a village of a 100 homesteads in the 15th century. Then it was a shadow of the powerful Roman city it had been. The triple-decker Pont du Gard gives advance warning as to its prestige during the classical era. Built in 19 BC it carried an aquaduct bearing spring water from the hills near Uzès.

The Marseillais author Marcel Pagnol picnicked by the arches of the Pont du Gard when he was a boy and Lawrence Durrell, a long-time resident in the Camargue, used it in his novel *Quinx* as the setting for a Baroque feast. Its centrepiece, created by the 'Great Nîmes chef, Tortoni' is 'a recumbant woman fashioned in butter with trimmings uttered in caviar of several different provenances and helpings of *saumon fumé* and an archipelago of iced potato salad to round out the offering. Venus rising from a Recamier of Baltic caviar' – perfect Provençal fare!

The Romans must have been glad of the cool spring water which flowed into their town. Nîmes is a dusty city, even today. But on Monday, 3rd October 1988 a dense black cloud hung over it. Early in the morning the rain started to pelt down with the ferocity of a tropical storm. In three hours, 30 cm fell. Flash floods raged down from the *garrigues* north and west of the city. Torrents of water coursed through the streets. Trees were uprooted; paving stones were torn up. Buses floated out of control. Cars were lifted and dumped in the canal surrounding the Jardins de la Fontaine. The Roman arena filled like a bath tub.

When the tide subsided, it left a shattered cityscape of broken houses, shops, junked vehicles, streets choked with tangled furniture and drowned bodies. On the excavated site of a planned arts centre an artificial reservoir nearly 20 metres deep had been created. The surface of Nîmes, ancient monuments and modern precincts, was smeared with a layer of mud flecked with oil and fuel. President Mitterand, visiting the city the day after the flood had to listen to tales of rats deserting the sewers and looters scavenging.

Coming to the city from Avignon, a month to the day after an event treated by the French Government as a national disaster, I had expected to find a shambles. Instead, the pavement cafés on the Boulevard Victor Hugo were spilling over with life. Shops seemed untainted. The Maison Carrée, a Roman temple, had survived the deluge as it had survived every other mishap over the last 2000 years, unscathed.

Antique monuments apart, Nîmes is more vibrant than pretty. Until the Revolution, it was a *Huguenot* stronghold, suffering religious persecution, at a time when Avignon, its neighbour, fattened on the protection and prosperity due to a Vatican colony. The contrast between the rival cities is still apparent. Even though Nîmes, a product of the railway age, has more inhabitants and no shortage of industry, its buildings are more provincial, its shops and restaurants less showy.

The city's arms display a crocodile chained to a palm tree. It symbolizes Augustus Caesar's defeat of Cleopatra and Mark Anthony, in which Gaulish auxiliary troops played a role and for which they were rewarded with land around Nîmes. Bronze studs, *clous*, bearing the image of a rather smug looking croc are stamped into the pavements of the main shopping streets. An excellent chocolate maker in the Boulevard Victor Hugo, *Moyne-Bressand*, sells glossy chocolate lozenges bearing its imprint. These *Clous de Nîmes*, filled with a bitter chocolate truffle mixture are flavoured with a fortified wine known as Carthagène. The name has a sound Provençal pedigree: in Châteauneuf-du-Pape peasants made a drink of that name by blending a quarter measure of the local alcohol, marc, with three parts of freshly pressed grape juice.

G. Moyne-Bressand
20 BOULEVARD VICTOR-HUGO
NIMES

Avignon's top restaurant is unpretentiously situated above a shoe shop.

The modern, branded version, created by a wine-grower in the Gard, is a pleasant enough aperitif tasting of muscat grapes, but hardly the real McCoy.

Moyne-Bressand also stamps a chained crocodile on a honey and almond biscuit. This is its version of another Nîmois speciality, the *Croquant Villaret*, made at the bakery of that name in the Rue de la Madeleine at the back of the cathedral. Villaret has baked its biscuits in the same oven since 1775.

Brandade de morue, the purée of salt cod and olive-oil which features in *Hiély-Lucullus*'s menu, predates these biscuits by at least 200 years. François I is said to have eaten it when he passed through the city early in the 16th century, but the dish may be as old as Nîmes itself. Salt was exported from the Rhône Delta both by sea and overland during the Roman occupation of Gaul. It was an ingredient of the mysterious liquefied fish seasoning, *garum*, which is thought to have resembled the Thai sauce *nam pla*. Containers discovered in Brittany prove that salt was also used to preserve fish.

Cod is not a Mediterranean fish. It probably first arrived with the Norsemen's longships. They filleted their fish, then air dried them until they grew hard as wood. They took these fish sticks, or *stokkfisk*, with them on their raids and foraging trips throughout the civilized world. Some stockfish found its way into Languedoc and Provence where it was called *Estocafic* or *Estofi*.

At the end of the Middle Ages, fishermen discovered the cod-rich grounds off Newfoundland. To bring back their catch in palatable form, they needed salt. Boats which travelled to Aigues-Mortes, 30 km south of Nîmes, brought with them fish salted on their previous journey to barter for the salt they needed for their next expedition. This *morue*, rather than the stockfish, is the basis of a modern *brandade*.

Morue is a feature of every Provençal market. The finest quality is plump and creamy white, its surface encrusted with a sheen of salt crystals, sparkling in the sunlight. Stockfish looks as though it should be used as a lethal weapon. It's wrinkled, buff and split like a kipper. Both require prolonged soaking in several changes of water to soften the flesh and extract the salt. One French Deputy kept the stockfish in the cistern of his toilet, so that he helped to desalt it every time he pulled the chain. When it is ready for the pot, the cod has become as bland as when it was first caught and the cook has to salt the water in which he poaches it. The first time I tried to prepare *brandade*, I mistakenly bought stockfish thinking it was *morue*. Following the instruction of my recipe, I left it 24 hours in water and wondered why it was still like old leather. Stockfish requires four days' immersion before it is ready for the pot.

Nîmes owes its name to a spring of fresh water which rises in the Jardin de la Fontaine. The Gauls identified it with a guardian spirit they called Nemet. This changed to Nemausus under the Romans and then to Nismes. Had the first inhabitants chanced on another source 12 km south-west of their settlement, close to the present village of Vergèze, they would have been astounded to discover that it disgorged a liquid producing a strange tickling sensation in the mouth. Closer inspection would have shown them that this was caused by a myriad of tiny bubbles. They would have discovered l'eau so famous, Perrier.

6

SALT, SAND AND WINDMILLS

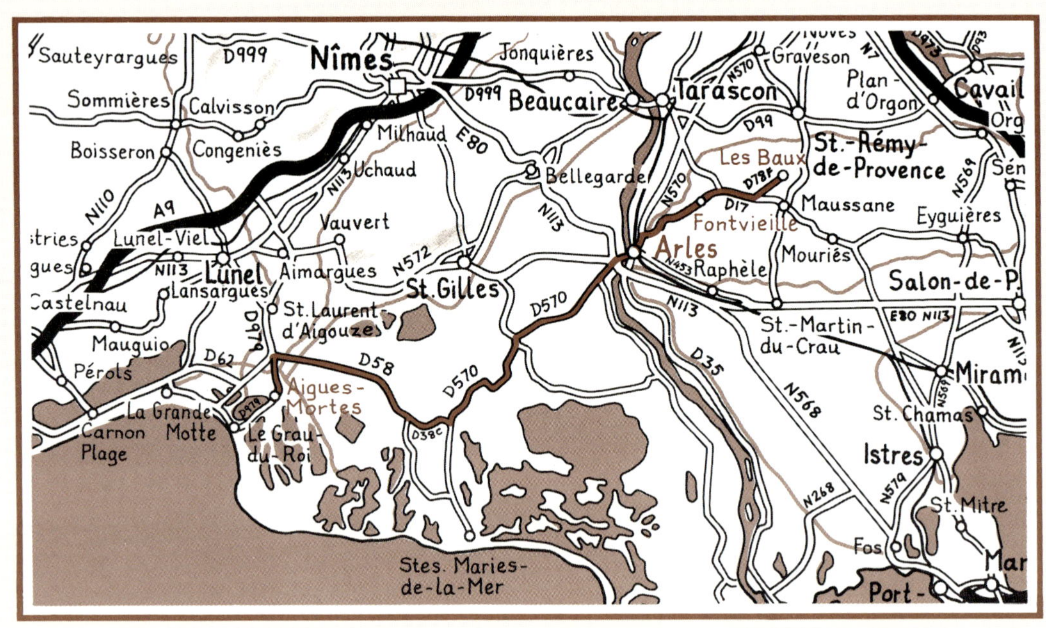

Aigues-Mortes – Arles – Fontvieille – Les Baux

At Nîmes, I boarded a creaking, crowded SNCF Autorail. It lurched south, skirting the Camargue in an awkward slalom, stopped at every hamlet en route and arrived finally at a run-down station outside the walls of Aigues-Mortes.

The town's medieval ramparts have remained intact like a perfect toy castle. From outside, the walls seem massive and daunting. That they have survived is due less to their being impregnable than to their being indefensible once cannons had been invented. Any competent military engineer could have breached the ten-metre-high walls in a day. Even during the Hundred Years War, the town changed hands on several occasions. In 1418, when it was held by Burgundians, the besieging Armagnac forces surprised and massacred the entire garrison. Their corpses were piled into a tower, the Tour des Bourguignons, and – to prevent their putrefaction – salted like cod.

Entering Aigues-Mortes through the main Porte de la Gardette is a thrill, even when you know that afterwards you will have to run the gauntlet of gypsy pizza merchants and curio shops in the Rue Jean Jaurès. In autumn, when the holidaymakers have left and the town reverts to its natural role of sleepy village with a communist mayor, it also regains its silence and dignity. The inner perimeter of the ramparts, sparsely lit after dark is stark and oppressive. Many of the shops and bars are shuttered. Cards in windows advertise rooms and apartments to let.

I stayed overnight at a comfortable restaurant with rooms, *Les Arcades*, in the Boulevard (big name for a little street) Gambetta. I dined on *boeuf à la gardiane* in a room divided by massive stone arches with a wooden ceiling supported on oak joists. The beef theoretically comes from the lyre-horned black Camarguais bulls which are kept on the 50 odd *manades* or ranches. They are reared less for their meat than for bullfighting. Aggressive bulls are revered for their courage, and rarely end up in the pot. It's the gentler unaggressive creatures which get cut into large chunks, marinated in red *Costières du Gard* wine and simmered till tender with olives and carrots.

The result is a dark brown stew. My portion was generous to a fault, designed for a real *gardian*, someone who had spent a day in the saddle, riding across the salt marshes, rather than an overfed traveller who had already enjoyed a good lunch.

Les Arcades
23 BOULEVARD GAMBETTA
30220 AIGUES-MORTES
TELEPHONE 66 53 81 13

In the morning, I met the patronne Marie-Pierre Merquiol and thanked her for supper. I asked her whether there were other typical Camarguais recipes. Not on her menu, she said, but she had had an aunt who used to make a *rouille blanche*, which was different from the hot, peppery mayonnaise served with fish soup along the length of the coast. As she described it, it was a mixture of potatoes and slightly rancid cuttlefish pounded to a paste and mixed with *aïoli*. Her aunt also had a special way with snails, which she called '*Caragoullettes*': 'You salt them till they have finished dribbling, then you put them in cold water and heat it gently until they pop their heads out their shells. Turn up the flame then to kill them while they are still on the outside. After that you cook them as usual with herbs, drain them and serve them with a vinaigrette containing plenty of herbs and garlic.'

A short Provençal moral tale on the subject of snails relates how they came to be considered gourmet food. Once upon a time they were considered to be only a pest because of the damage they caused to vines. A vinegrower put up a large sign saying: 'Anyone caught stealing my snails will be prosecuted'. His neighbour approached him and queried: 'Why should anybody want to pinch your snails?' The farmer gave him a cryptic but knowing look, arched his eyebrows and replied, 'Don't be so naïve.' After that the number of snails on the vinegrower's property began to diminish and within months they were beginning to appear on the menus of the most fashionable tables in the region.

An inhabitant of Aigues-Mortes who stood on the newly built walls of his town in about 1300 and gazed south would have seen a sheltered bay open to the Mediterranean. Sand and silt and salt have blocked its entrance, creating a ribbon of dry land. The dead waters under the ramparts today are bounded by marshes to the east and by the salt beds of the Compagnie des Salins du Midi which owns all the land, about 20,000 acres of it, south of the town.

Salt has been a local industry ever since an engineer, Peccius, began extracting it at the height of the Roman Empire. In the Middle Ages, the Abbots of Psalmodi and the local land-barons who controlled the salt production operated a comfortable cartel which determined the measures used for selling the salt. They also reached a formal agreement on labour relations; a serf sacked from on one property would not be re-employed by the other. After the Middle Ages, the Peccais salt-beds (named after the Roman engineer) were operated as a number of small private businesses, which eventually combined to run as a co-operative. During the Revolution, the Republic took over the Salins, but returned them two years later.

Salins du Midi, the company which dominates France's modern sea-salt manufacturing industry evolved out of the co-operative. When it acquired the Giraud salt pans at the other end of the Rhône delta by Port-St-Louis, it controlled a natural resource which supplies a million tonnes of salt a year.

At Aigues-Mortes the salt-beds cover an area larger than Paris. Sea-water is channelled into a tracery of shallow ponds linked by hundreds of kilometres of dykes. As the wind and sun evaporate the water, the brine's density of sodium chloride is concentrated to ten times its original strength. It's then pumped into one of 50 rectangular basins, the smallest one several times as big as a football pitch, and left to dry out through the summer. When it's ready for harvesting the salt layer, about 10 cm deep, and looking as though it had been spread on a frosty road, is scraped off its bed and carted off in dumper trucks for purification. The ponds are a favourite haunt for the colony of flamingos which lives in the Camargue.

During October, at the rate of 15,000 tonnes a day, the year's harvest is piled into an off-white mountain of salt, over 20 metres high, to be scooped away as the year progresses.

Not all the land owned by the Salins du Midi can be turned to the business of salt. Three prime ribs of sandy soil running through the beds have been used for over a century to grow vines. To reduce the land's salinity, the wine growers flush fresh water from the Rhône through the fields twice a year. The wines, sold under the brand name, *Listel*, are more than a curiosity. Vines cover a quarter of the area owned by the company in the Petit Camargue. Listel's winery at Aigues-Mortes holds half a million gallons of red, white, rosés and sparkling '*Vins des Sables*'. They are all meant to be drunk young and the fresh white *Domaine de Villervy*, is made like the best Muscadets of the Loire, by bottling the wine directly from the casks without racking it – producing a slightly prickly quality. As an alternative to the hundreds of ordinary Côtes de Provence, Listel wines make splendid holiday quaffing.

You can buy Listel wines at:

Chais de Vieillissement du Listel

DOMAINE DE JARRAS

30220 AIGUES-MORTES

TELEPHONE 66 53 63 65

Just outside Aigues-Mortes, heading for Arles I hitched a ride from a disc jockey in one of the town's night spots. His discotheque earnings had given him the money to buy a white Camarguais stallion. It had not cost him a lot, about 1500 francs, but he spent more feeding it and looking after it than he did on his car. The wild horses which roam the Camargue feed off the tamarisk and marsh samphire (which is popular as a garnish on the platters of gourmet restaurants along the coast), but his required its oats.

He wondered whether I had drunk in the *Express Bar* in the Place St Louis. 'It's the hub of the town,' he told me, 'only you don't say you are going to the *Express*, you say you are going to *La Soute*. It's run by a lady well into her eighties; it's dirty; it hasn't been repainted for ten years, but it's got more atmosphere than all the other bars put together.' *La Soute* approximates to 'coal-hole'.

What was the in drink in the bars?

In his club it was a *Perroquet*, a dangerous blend of *pastis* and *menthe*. If I had been in Aigues-Mortes for the Festival I could have enjoyed or observed its effects. It's a week-long party, held in October, to celebrate the salt and wine harvests. The town's ten gates are thrown open, a trumpet blows and black bulls run through the streets. Between the horns are rosettes and around them cords which young *razeteurs* attempt to lift. Teams of youths club together during the year to buy a beat-up car which they use to hunt the bull. They probably run more risk of injury driving than from their quarry.

The road into Arles (D570) passed between paddy fields. Although rice plays less of a role in the Camargue's economy than salt, the ecological link between the cereal and the mineral goes back a long way. The plantations served to complete the annexation of the marshes from the sea, at the same time desalinating the newly acquired land. Rice did not figure in the routine diet of Arlesiens. A researcher would scan the old cookery treatises in vain for the equivalent of a *paella* or *risotto*. For the most part, the cereal was fodder for livestock.

In the 1950s, before Parisians developed a taste for Uncle Ben's, the Camargue supplied enough rice to meet the national demand. But it was a short-grained pudding rice, not much good for savoury dishes. The production declined by over half,

One of Arles' claims to fame is its sausage.

replaced by cash crops more in demand, such as sunflowers and rape which provide much of France's cooking oil. The economic pendulum has swung once more, and rice is again being planted. Longer grain varieties with a nutty flavour are replacing the rounder types.

Many of the new generation of farmers grow it and dry it organically, instead of processing an asceptic *riz à l'Americaine*. Their paddies are irrigated by a network of canals which pump water to them from the Little Rhône. During the earlier boom the levels of pesticides and herbicides which drained from the *rizières*, had threatened the balance of nature in the Camargue, especially in the Etang de Vaccarès, a Regional Nature Reserve. Now there is a tenuous entente between agriculture, the salt industry and conservationists.

The disc jockey dropped me, and a horse breeder from Fourques drove me the few remaining kilometres into Arles. Apart from its Roman arena, the Arlesienne, and its association with Vincent Van Gogh, Arles is famous for its sausage. 'Watch out,' my chauffeur told me, 'there is genuine and there is phoney.' The characteristic of the *saucisson d'Arles* is its leanness. Pigs were never a commercial proposition for peasants who kept one pig which they fattened and killed in autumn. But on the Crau plain, east of the city, herds of horses, bulls and donkeys roamed alongside the flocks of sheep, and these red meats with little fat formed the basis of the Arles sausage. The problem with the flesh was that it dehydrated in the months that it took for the *saucisson* to dry. Once the local charcutiers found pork readily available, they preferred to use it because they would obtain twice as much *saucisson* for the same weight of raw material.

Genin
RUE DES PORCELETS
13200 ARLES

M. Lautier recommended me to buy a brand called *Farandola* from the charcuterie *Genin*. He said that it contained the essential ingredient, donkey meat. Having tasted donkey *saucisson* on the market at L'Isle-sur-la-Sorgue, I was not too shocked by the dry, gamey taste.

The charcuterie is at the bottom of the appropriately named Rue des Porcelets. According to a local legend, the Countess of Castille, who was living in the town, refused alms to an old hag. At that moment, a sow walked by, and the witch put a curse on the noble lady so that she would give birth to as many children as the sow had in a litter. Afterwards, the countess gave birth to a string of piglets. What actually happened was that the countess gave birth to seven sons, one of whom became the Marquis de Porcelet.

To obtain some measure of comparison, I also bought some *saucisson* from another butcher, *Pierre Milhau*, in the Rue Réattu. His version was much closer to a charcutier's *saucisson sec*, made with plenty of pork – but he assured me that he did put a small proportion of donkey meat into it. Where did the donkey come from? After all, they are not that common a sight in Provence, let alone the Camargue.

'Getting hold of it is the hardest part,' the butcher claimed. 'Most of what we buy comes from Corsica.'

Authenticity apart, I preferred eating M. Milhau's sausage because, to be honest, I couldn't detect a flavour of old donkey. Some regional specialities, such as *saucisson d'Arles*, which originated because of local circumstances may find it hard to survive when those circumstances have changed. For the record, the original *saucisson d'Arles* was not created by a Provençal or even a Frenchman. It was concocted by a pork butcher from Bologna who was working in Arles.

That did not prevent Frédéric Mistral from describing it to the great chef, Escoffier, as the centrepiece of the hors d'oeuvre at a special Arlesian dinner he arranged. 'As a curtain raiser hors d'oeuvre, a real jumble of Provençal goodies over which the fine Saucisson d'Arles presided; then came a crayfish tart perfect as Santo-Estello, followed by a mountain of frogs' legs from Maillane, fried in virgin oil, surrounded with sautéed cèpes and cloves of garlic cooked in the ashes, the whole covered with chopped parsley.'

Frogs' legs, alas, if they appear on a Provençal menu nowadays will probably have been imported frozen from the Indian sub-continent. Crayfish, on offer in most restaurants from which it would be impossible to escape for less than 500 francs, are imported live from Turkey or Bulgaria. There is a small river curling around the small town of Barjols to the east of Aix, known as the Ruisseau des Ecrivisses (Crayfish Stream). Naïvely, I inquired of a farmer how the locals went about catching and cooking these delicacies. 'You'll be lucky,' he said. 'We haven't seen any crayfish there for years.'

Au Roi du Charolais

PIERRE MILHAU

11 RUE REATTU

13200 ARLES

TELEPHONE 90 96 16 05

A mountain of salt in the Camargue.

Daudet's Mill. Local restaurants exploit its literary connections.

Museon Arlaten
RUE DE LA REPUBLIQUE
13200 ARLES
TELEPHONE 90 96 08 23

Mistral's Provence is very different from today's. The *Museon Arlaten* which he created with money from his Nobel Prize for Literature in 1896, is the closest, barring his writing, that most of us can come to it. The museum is a strange building of echoing corridors, dark galleries and exhibits ranging from kitchens to cockle scrapers. It has whistles made out of peach stones and traps for catching eels from Martigues. There are tridents for spearing fish, and spiral-glazed plates from Moustiers near the Lac de Sainte Croix.

In one particularly dusty cabinet is a row of shells of four edible snails, laid out on some greying crushed leaves. The largest, a Coutat, is almost the size of the escargot de Bourgogne, France's largest edible snail. Next down is a Cacalan; it bears a footnote that it can be eaten without first being purged. The third snail is a Mourgeto and the smallest, a white snail, called a Meissounenco, after the Provençal word for 'harvest'. Beside them is a tool made from a carob spine which looks as though it ought to be an awl but which was used to extract the snails from their shells. The museum also exhibits a *cacalausiero*, a vase for snails, where they were left to purge before cooking.

The *Museon Arlaten* pulled me in different directions. Part of me, the modern man, was thinking that this musty relic needed a good face-lift; there is one modern gallery tucked away on an upper floor which highlights the sense of walking through a mausoleum elsewhere. But I also felt that the place was the poet's shrine, set out as he wanted it, showing Provence as he had experienced it. If it were dismantled and reassembled as a stylish folk museum so as to render it more 'accessible', more 'interesting', more informative, then it would be a sign that the old Provence had finally succumbed.

Le Pinède
M. ET MME FLECHON
13990 FONTVIEILLE

Through the *Syndicat d'Initiative* in Arles I booked a bed and breakfast room. *Le Pinède* is a modern villa set back from the main road on the edge of Fontvieille. The French have come late to B & B; it isn't always cheap, it's not signposted, and turning up without a booking can lead to disappointment. But it can be as comfortable as a luxury hotel. After Madame had calmed her Alsatian and its smaller assistant guard dog, she showed me to a small suite with stained glass windows, bunches of dried flowers on every available surface and a bed which could be raised or lowered at both ends for extra comfort. In the bathroom was a small basket filled with corked vials containing essences of lavender and balm.

The house was 15 minutes' walk from the village. Fontvieille marks the outpost leading to the ruined citadel of Les Baux. In season, it's an outsize parking lot, filled with trippers come to pay their respects to a disused windmill, set among parasol pines. It's known as the *Moulin de Daudet*, Daudet's Mill, after the author of a famous set of short stories, *Lettres de Mon Moulin*, read at school by every French child. Despite the title, Alphonse Daudet wrote the book in Paris and never owned the mill – although he had visited it often when staying with friends in Provence.

It was operational in his day, one of three mills producing flour from the cereals which were grown in the neighbourhood of Fontvieille, but shut down during the Great War. Daudet's Mill has been preserved, but the two other windmills on a facing knoll have lost the conical wooden lantern-towers to which the sails were attached. To catch the wind the miller turned the lantern until the sails were in position, then locked it into place in one of 32 notches, each one corresponding to a wind. The notch for the Mistral points North-West. Others have lesser known but equally evocative names: Mango Fango, Narbounes, Auro Rousso, Tremountano.

To exploit the connection with the *Lettres de Mon Moulin*, local restaurateurs have drawn on the most famous story in the book, *Monsieur Seguin's Goat*. It's the tale of a young goat, *un chèvre*, who fights an all-night battle with a wolf, *un loup*, until the sun rises when the wolf eats it. Almost every menu advertises a *salade verte au chèvre chaud*, salad with 'hot goat', or *loup à l'anis*, or *mousseline de loup*. Contrary to appearances the Fontvieillois have not tracked down a source of wolf meat as the Arlesian butchers have donkey. 'Loup' in this case is a sea-wolf, the Mediterranean name for sea-bass. Boned, stuffed and encased in puff pastry, served with a crayfish sauce, *loup en croûte* has been a showpiece at *L'Oustau de Beaumanière*, the restaurant at Les Baux, for over a decade.

Fontvieille has another less visible mill, the *Moulin de Bédarrides*, at the end of a farm track near the old railway line. It produces not flour but oil, and of a very different character from those pressed in Nyons. Henri Bellon, the owner, presses Salanenque olives which have been picked green rather than the mature black Tanches

Buy prize-winning olive-oil at:

Moulin de Bédarrides

HENRI BELLON

13990 FONTVIEILLE

TELEPHONE 90 97 70 04

(Remote, but worth a detour)

or

Coopérative Oléicole de la Vallée des Baux

13520 MAUSSANE LES ALPILLES

TELEPHONE 90 97 32 37

of Nyons. In an ancient-looking barn, he has installed modern equipment which removes any leaves, washes, crushes and minces the olives before separating the oil ready for bottling.

Monsieur Bellon is proud of his oils, which are almost emerald green and extremely fruity. He displays the gold medals which they have won for three generations. His big rival is the *Coopérative Oléicole de la Vallée des Baux* in Maussane, to the east of Fontvieille, which consistently scores the highest marks in blind tastings of French oils. But oils are personal like scent. Ideally, we might keep a dark cupboard full of various oils, for different moods, different dishes, different occasions.

Whether all the olives which are grist to the Bellon or Co-op mills originated on the slopes around Les Baux or even in France is another matter. A guide at Daudet's Mill told me that olives earn nothing for local farmers. There are fewer trees than ever, and the crops are irregular. As an ancient privilege, Fontvieillois still enjoy the right to glean for olives in any farmer's groves within the commune, after the harvest has finished. These pickings were taken to mills and earned a few extra *sous* for the poor. Now, even these left-overs are not worth taking.

La Régalido
RUE F. MISTRAL
13990 FONTVIEILLE
TELEPHONE 90 97 70 17

Fontvieille has another 'moulin'. *Le Régalido*, a chic hotel-restaurant converted from an oil mill, belongs to a prestige consortium *Relais et Châteaux* which sets out to group together the best and most elegant establishments in France. This select professional club guarantees the level of comfort expected by sophisticated travellers and often food to match.

But within the *Relais et Châteaux* organization, there are grades reflecting different levels of prestige. Some 12 kilometres from Fontvieille, at Les Baux-de-Provence, is another ex-oil mill, *L'Oustau de Beaumanière*. This, you may remember, is where Micäel Reboul in Ménerbes had trained, and where the *loup en croûte* still stars. It provides the kind of surroundings and luxury which reduce *Régalido*, by comparison, to the level of a small country hostelry.

Raymond Thuilier, who 'founded' *L'Oustau de Beaumanière*, bought it during the Second World War and ran it for 40 years, well in to his eighties. It has been crowned with three Michelin stars since 1954. Despite the price – a meal here will cost about 1000 francs – restaurants of this calibre earn less revenue from the food they sell than

Drinking pastis with old friends – a favourite Provençal pastime.

L'Oustau de Beaumanière
AU VAL D'ENFER
LES BAUX-DE-PROVENCE
TELEPHONE 90 97 33 07

from merchandising. They have had to learn how to squeeze every last drop from their celebrity by selling anything from bath robes monogrammed with their logo to pots of jam. *L'Oustau de Beaumanière*, for instance, sells its own oil, not such a stark green as M. Bellon's or as fine as the Co-op's, but good nonetheless.

It also runs a wine club for past guests of the hotel from a small warehouse in Fontvieille. It's an astute scheme and an attractive one, because the wines which feature on the list cost so much less than in the restaurant. Buying them costs little more than acquiring them from a reputable shipper and, of course, there is the cachet of knowing that the wines have been specially selected for their quality. The club's list has oddities such as the *Domaine de Trévallon* produced in the shadow of Les Baux, rarities such as a red *Hermitage Les Mandouls* produced by Michel Ferraton in a vineyard of about five acres and delicacies such as L'Oustau's house champagne, *Réserve Spéciale Raymond Thuilier*, made from juice extracted by the weight of grapes in the vat before the first pressing.

After salivating over the club's list, I thought long and hard before deciding not to go to *L'Oustau de Beaumanière*. M. Reboul's criticism in Ménerbes did not influence me; in fact Jean-André Chariel, who has taken over the hotel from his grandfather, has improved its gastronomic reputation. But I felt that to go there now, with no special appetite for luxury at a table for one, would have served little purpose other than to cross a famous name off a hypothetical list of places that ought to be visited.

Instead I popped into a Fontvieille café opposite the post office. It was seven o'clock. In a row, about a dozen men stood drinking pastis in small, careful gulps. These were serious drinkers for the most part, who added only a splash of water to their aniseed aperitif and swallowed four or five in half an hour. Some ordered Ricard, more Pernod, like kids who will drink Coke rather than Pepsi and vice versa.

The multinational Pernod-Ricard stable distils both alcohols. Although the sweet aniseed liquors have become the quintessential Mediterranean man's tipple, they are both 20th-century inventions which evolved from *absinthe*. A Dr Pernod bought the original absinthe recipe from a Frenchman living in Switzerland during the Napoleonic wars and his name became synonymous with it. When this was banned early this century on the grounds that too much of it caused brain damage, the Pernod firm switched to a less noxious concoction, yellow rather than green, and it was 'Business as usual'. Soon after the Great War, a M. Ricard started hawking his eponymous beverage round the bistros of Marseille. The two brands competed with each other and were eventually merged under Ricard's control.

With Marseille my next port of call, this seemed as good a moment to toast M. Ricard's health. I took my place at the bar, watched the yellow alcohol in my glass turn cloudy, sipped it and mused as to whether I was missing the meal of a lifetime.

7

BACK-STREET FOOD

Marseille – Cassis – Marseille (again) – L'Estaque – Martigues

After the pink flamingos, white horses and black bulls of the Camargue, Marseille, France's second largest city, provides a striking counterpoint. The train from Arles hums briefly across the fertile strip of the Crau plain, skirts the Etang de Berre – once a hunter's paradise, now a petrochemical soup – and dips into the city.

Marseille has always been tough, dirty and cussed – Romans called it the biggest whorehouse in the Mediterranean – but it thrums to that indefinable pulse which drives most great seaports. Its inhabitants, too, have the bitter-sweet humour which thrives on hardship, as well as an inveterate streak of sentimentality.

Marcel Pagnol, born in the satellite town of Aubagne, captured this blend of hard crust and soft centre in his play *Marius*. First performed in 1929, it's about a young man from Marseille who dreams of escaping his father's bar to go to sea. He falls in love, hesitates to leave, but finally makes the break – abandoning Fanny, the girl who minds the oyster stall next to the bar on the quayside of Marseille's Vieux-Port.

Whatever Marseille was like then, it seems to have lost its innocence. The loud-mouthed César, Marius's father, who opens his bar at three in the morning and whose worst crime is that he can't resist a little good-natured cheating at cards with his friends, has been superseded, if *Le Provençal*'s hype is to be believed, by the gangster patrons of the Pizza Connection. The local paper's centre spread is a heavy slurry of topical crime: cigarette smugglers laundering cash from prostitution; American girls raped; a Molotov cocktail thrown into an immigrant hostel; six hold-ups in 48 hours – one outside a bank; one at a drugstore; one at a hairdresser's; one at a red traffic light and two at bakeries. That may be a sordid veneer, bearing little relationship to life as it is lived by 99 per cent of the city's upright citizens, but the surface impression counts to a visitor.

Bars like César's in and around the Vieux-Port have changed less over the last 60 years than the port itself. Gone are the mountains of groundnuts and cartons bearing the names of 'Bangkok, Batavia and Sydney' which seduced Marius. The swaying masts belong, not to clippers bound for distant shores, but to the rows of yachts which use it as a marina. A flotilla of pleasure boats bob at their moorings, waiting to shuttle trippers round the modern docks which run at right angles to the

Bistro Thiars
PLACE THIARS
MARSEILLE 1ER
TELEPHONE 91 54 03 94

old port or to the fortress of the Château d'If where Alexandre Dumas *Père*'s Count of Monte Cristo was held prisoner.

One day I shall muster enough courage to ask a Marseille barman on the Quai du Port to mix me César's special, a *picon-citron-curaçao*: 'First of all, you put a third of curaçao. Pay attention: a tiny third. Good. Now a third of lemon juice. A little bit larger. Good. Afterwards a GOOD third of Picon. Look at the colour. Look how pretty it is. And finally, a LARGE third of water. There you go.' Picon, a gentian-based syrup, is still available. A dash of it in beer is surprisingly GOOD.

Instead of attempting to recreate the fictional cocktail, I enjoyed a glass of white wine in the *Bistro Thiars* in a square off the Quai de Rive Neuve. Although it's close to the pizza- and burger-zone of central Marseille, this café has an almost Florentine feel to it. The terrace, with its cane chairs, overlooks a fountain, and the pastel toned facades in the square are decked with Virginia creeper. The bistro serves what might be termed Provençal *tapas*: garlic flavoured octopus, spicy mussels from Bouzigues in the Languedoc, aubergine fritters and squid in a tomato sauce.

Fanny's mother Honorine, a fishwife, would be dismayed by the seafood which is hawked from trestle tables along the Quai des Belges at the bottom of the Vieux-Port. It's fresh, no question of that. It's varied: bream, rascasse, gunards, red mullets, octopus and ormers to name just a few of the dozens of varieties. But there is so little of it. What's there is under-size, and much of it probably under the legal size too. The seven kilos of red mullet which Honorine sold in a day as a matter of course, even when the Mistral blew, would earn a week's wages today.

One of the ladies on the quay had a plastic box full of the coral coloured *opercula*, the round 'front doors' extracted from sea-snails. She called them St Lucy's eyes and sold them at 10 francs each as a good luck charm. In Provence, they are sometimes nicknamed *oreilles de St Pierre*, so by a curious juxtaposition of images, St Lucy's eyes act as plugs in St Peter's ears.

The smallest smolts sold on the trestle tables are rockfish which have been netted in the *calanques* or creeks between Cap Croisette, just south of the city, and Cap Canaille, near Cassis. They form the basis of *soupe de poisson à la marseillaise*. Flavoured with garlic, dried orange peel, fennel and saffron, it used to be eaten in winter when the cold Mistral wind blew. The taste is as good as the better known *bouillabaisse* and costs a fraction of the price in bistros. I like it best when it has been whizzed up in a food processor, a heresy which some Marseillais resent.

Nearly all the local catch sold in the *Poissonnerie des Halles*, at the fish market, or by the fishwives has been netted close to land by fishermen working from open *barqueroles*. From Marseille to Nice, it's the same story. In every port, the local fishermen's guild of *Pêcheurs Prud'hommes* may have several hundred members, but few earn a full-time living from their craft.

The closest equivalent of Fanny's oyster stand is the pair of 'mollusc merchants' whose pitch is the Cours St Louis off Marseille's main street, La Canebière. They sell oysters, clams and mussels from Bouzigues, but the local delicacy is a *Violet Rocher* or sea squirt. Alan Davidson, in *Mediterranean Seafood*, describes it as a knobbly creature with a leathery skin which lives anchored to rocks or the seabed. 'The ones,' he writes 'which I ate in Marseille certainly tasted quite good, and were fairly small. I have never faced up to a big one.' A large Violet sits snugly in the palm of the hand. Although 'leathery' is an understatement for the coarse, gnarled exterior, it is not made of shell like an oyster, nor does the *marchand de coquillages* have to prise it open; he slices it through the middle and the yellowish, curdy meat fills both halves. One large Violet is not an excessive snack, not even at eight o'clock in the morning when I sampled one, but the strong, very salty, iodine taste cries out for a glass of chilled wine.

Perhaps they are not meant to be street food. *Chi-chi fregi* is. It's a kind of doughnut, lighter than Spanish *churros*, though so similar that one wonders whether they do not both have the same ancestry. I bought mine from the one place in the centre of Marseille which still sells them. *Etape* is a corner shop half way up a narrow side street, the Rue d'Aubagne, which branches off the Cours St Louis, at the corner of the Rue Vacon. The *chi-chi* batter is fried in a basin like a wok. It's piped into the hot oil in a spiral, taken out when crisp, drained and dusted with sugar. You buy a length, roughly the thickness of a banana and eat it still hot.

The *chi-chi* man has another Marseille speciality, *panisse*, which several bakeries sell as a flat pudding. It's a springy type of polenta made from boiled chick-pea flour.

Fish market:

QUAI DES BELGES

Poissonnerie des Halles

7 AVENUE DU PRADO

MARSEILLE 6E

TELEPHONE 91 78 89 53

Etape

RUE D'AUBAGNE

MARSEILLE 1ER

A long sausage, the diameter of a hockey puck or a fish cake is sliced into rings or moulded and fried till golden. You can also buy it unfried, by the weight, to take away and cook at home.

Also in the Rue d'Aubagne is a spice shop, *Arax*, for those who cannot resist rummaging through sacks of paprika, or green peppercorns from Madagascar, or the finest Moroccan saffron, or real Turkish delight. The atmosphere is a bit like a warehouse, and nobody minds if you touch or sniff, or nibble at a date.

Marseille markets
AVENUE DU PRADO
PLACE CASTELLANE
PLACE DES CAPUCINS

Marseille has two dozen markets, and it would be reasonable to expect that Provence's capital attracted the pick of the crop. The largest, and probably the longest stretches for more than a kilometre along both sides of the Avenue du Prado. Maybe it was a case of not seeing the wood for the trees, but I was looked in vain for outstanding produce. Salads were less varied and less fresh than those in the markets at Cannes or Aix. Nearly all the fish and seafood had been brought in from outside the Mediterranean. Except for the odd garlic seller, there were none of the small, specialist traders, with a dozen jars of honey, or a few chickens in a cage, or a box of home-made cheeses, or pretty bottles of olive-oil containing sprigs of thyme or oregano and fastened with a pink ribbon which are the delight of so many other markets.

Even the fruit and vegetables seemed tired by comparison with the 'Arab market'. Located in a warren of alleys around the Place des Capucins, it had all the atmosphere of an Algerian souk. Strips of halal meat swung from hooks in butchers' shops opening directly on to the street. Piles of red and green capsicums, still grimy with soil from the fields were manhandled by a dozen pairs of African hands. Kadaif, Baclava, Kab el Ghazal and almond, pistachio or pine-kernel cakes lay in the windows of Moroccan patisseries.

The city's North African enclave has grown both in size and importance, stretching below the Gare St Charles in a sweeping crescent to the Cours Belsunce and across the Canebière. Since the first generation of Algerian immigrants arrived in the 1960s, attracted by the demand for cheap labour, many have climbed the socio-economic ladder. Savings garnered by working on building sites went to purchase shops and other small businesses.

An enthusiastic fishwife in Marseille's Vieux-Port.

Georges Bataille
18 RUE FONTANGE
MARSEILLE 6E
TELEPHONE 91 47 06 23

During the oil boom, Algerian middle-classes crossed the Mediterranean to shop in Marseille. Their spending-power fuelled Algerian-owned businesses and helped them to expand. Young entrepreneurs, such as Slimane Azzoug, who has become king of the Halal butchery trade, emerged. By the time the North African petro-dollars started to dry up, the Algerian community's role had gained enough momentum to sustain itself within the city's economic activity.

Although Marseille lays claim to being France's second city, it has none of the gastronomic riches of say, Lyon. The better food shops lie off the Place Jean-Jaurès. *Georges Bataille*'s has many of the more recherché Provençal specialities, cheeses especially (he is president of the regional branch of the *Guilde des Maître-Fromagers*). One tray, bearing rows of tiny goat cheeses, caught my eye. Some were round, others shaped like beehives, a third variety was a miniature pyramid and a forth, *doigts de fées* ('nimble fingers'), had a stalk sticking out of the top. I inquired of a rather stuffy *vendeuse* whether they all came from the same source, and received a severe school mam's look followed by a two minute lecture on how Monsieur Bataille bought each one from a different Lubéron farm. They all had a unique taste, it's true, ranging from fruity to almost sharp.

M. Bataille's 'cellar' shows off armagnac dating back to the middle of the last century, cognac from Napoleon III's special reserve and wines from nearly all of Provence's prestige estates. Upstairs, he stocks rows of oils, treating them like wines. They come from all the major and some unusual minor Provençal producers. There are nut oils made from pressed pistachios, walnuts and hazelnut as well as a *huile de pignons*, from pressed pine kernels.

Marseille has a rather bizarre local speciality. When the rest of France is eating pancakes, on February 2nd (Candlemas rather than Shrove Tuesday), people here go to a bakery close to the Basilica of St Victor. The long queue which forms is there to buy *navettes*, bone-shaped bun-biscuits – usually by the dozen.

How the Basilica and the bone-shaped bun-biscuit come to be related to each other is an obscure and convoluted story. Early in the Middle Ages, a crowned statue of a black Virgin washed up on a beach and became a cult figure for the Marseillais. Some worshipped her as the Seafarers' Virgin who protected sailors. Others called her Notre Dame du Feu Nouveau, Our Lady of the New Fire. In this capacity, she was paraded round the Place St Victor every year at Candlemas. The archbishop blessed the sea, the port and the town and the statue was returned to storage in the crypt for another year.

Over the following eight days, Masses were sung, the faithful lit green candles, a privilege of the Abbey of St Victor, and afterwards they bought a dozen *navettes*. Nobody knows which baker invented them or, to be honest, what they represent. In its original sense a *navette* is a shuttle used for weaving, but it is also the word used to describe a liturgical incense carrier. Another suggestion is that the *navettes* which have splits down the middle and bobbles at either end represent the boat which brought the first Saints to Provence. Rather more far-fetched is a suggestion that it is a symbol of Isis.

The bakery, *Four des Navettes* in the Rue Sainte, has a tradition of baking these curious biscuits since 1781. They used to be made during the one week, but now they can be bought throughout the year. The recipe is intended to be a secret, but it's a bit like a dry, sweet brioche, flavoured with orange and lemon. According to the baker, Rudy Caumont, they keep for up to a year, rather like a ship's biscuit. Perhaps that throws another light on their origins.

Authentic or not, the *navette's* shape has been borrowed by several Marseille bakers. One of them, *Georges Michel* in the Rue Vacon, makes an organic, wholefood version. Although that may be something of a gimmick, there is nothing phoney about his breads, which include a loaf containing spelt, a semi-wild wheat variety, and anchovy *fougasses* prepared from leaven.

A Master Baker, M. Michel condemned the chain bread shops in the city which receive ready-to-bake doughs which are merely baked on-site. Underlying his criticism was an unspoken fear that technology was undermining his craft, that one day soon customers would no longer be able to distinguish between the genuine article and the copy.

Another bakery, *Mandonato* in the Rue Breteuil, enjoys the reputation of baking the best *Poumpo*, the centrepiece of the '13 Desserts' (which don't have to number 13!) which traditionally end every Provençal Christmas feast. It's not that different

Four des Navettes
136 RUE SAINTE
MARSEILLE 1ER
TELEPHONE 91 33 32 12

Georges Michel
33 RUE VACON
MARSEILLE 1ER
TELEPHONE 91 33 79 43

Mandonato
8 RUE BRETEUIL
MARSEILLE 1ER
TELEPHONE 91 33 26 40

from other yeast cakes, such as brioche, except that oil replaces butter. The dough is moulded and scored on top, so that when it rises, a regular pattern of bumps decorates the surface. And the other desserts? Raisins; dried figs; almonds; walnuts; oranges; dates; nougat; candied fruit from Apt; roast chestnuts from Collobrières; apples, and pears.

Bouillabaisse attracts more myth and more mystique than any other culinary landmark. The only point about which there is a measure of agreement is that the fish stew to end all fish stews derives from Marseille. Beyond that let battle commence. To protect the honour of their celebrated dish, a group of Marseillais restaurateurs has banded together and created a Bouillabaisse Charter.

The Charter stipulates that the composition should include at least four varieties of fish from the following list: Rascasse, White rascasse, Weever, John Dory, Monkfish, Conger eel and Scorpion fish, adding that the list should make allowances for landings and the number of diners. 'One essential fact that remains for the quality of a bouillabaisse,' it concludes, 'is the extreme freshness of the fish, the primordial condition of its success.'

Although there is general agreement on the sense of the word *bouillabaisse* (boil/lower [the heat]), it's interpreted by Marseillais cooks in two ways. One school believes that the broth must be taken off the boil and allowed to simmer before adding the fish; the other argues that the broth comes off the boil because the temperature drops when the fish is added. In either case the boiling part is important, because it helps the water to amalgamate with the olive-oil, which would otherwise lie on top of the soup like a slick. A third chapter, the colonials of Martigues, a fishing port which is almost a suburb of Marseille nowadays, puts all the ingredients in the pot together, boils them hard and then lets the fish finish cooking over a more gentle flame.

There is almost as much flim-flam about the service of a *bouillabaisse* and the accompaniments presented with it. The Charter states: 'It is a fundamental rule that the fish should be filleted and served in front of the customers.' Presumably, if they were left to do it themselves, there would be fights as to who gets which piece of fish. This sanitized form of eating makes it virtually impossible to do what the

A good catch of fish is becoming much less common.

Le Bacon

BOULEVARD DE BACON

06600 CAP D'ANTIBES

TELEPHONE 93 61 50 02

(Closed from November to end of January)

fishermen can do openly in the privacy of their homes: suck the fish heads, most of which contain succulent tit-bits of flesh, John Dory especially, and sometimes sweet gelatinous juices (rascasse). There may be a more prosaic reason. Many rockfish have sharp, even venomous spines, which could ruin the most robust appetite if one lodged in a diner's throat.

Traditionally, *bouillabaisse* was served with dry bread rubbed with garlic and *rouille*, a garlic mayonnaise sauce, like *aïoli*, to which hot pepper is added. The restaurant dish usually has fried croutons of sliced baguette, a bowl of *aïoli*, one of *rouille* and another of grated gruyère, all of which adds to the performance without contributing overmuch to the end-product.

Notwithstanding the Charter, I think that anyone who goes to Marseille determined to eat a *bouillabaisse* needs to follow a few, simple ground rules. One, don't go alone; it's a family dish and needs to be lavish; lunching alone, I've tasted a pleasant little fish stew at *Chez Madie* on the Quai du Port but it did not deserve the name of *bouillabaisse*. Two, have a good sniff when you go in the restaurant; it should smell of herbs and saffron and fresh fish stock. Three, check the price. Four demand to see the fish before you order and reject any not having bright eyes. On second thoughts, if any have sunken eyes eat somewhere else. Don't order a *bouillabaisse* which has a crawfish in it; it probably comes from Brittany and will double the bill.

Finally, if you want the best *bouillabaisse* on the Côte, and money is no object, book a table at *Le Bacon* at Cap d'Antibes, overlooking the Baie des Anges. The fish restaurant which Alphonsine Sordello started over 30 years ago, and has since passed to her sons, really does live up to expectations. Didi Sordello never overcooks the fish, which is one of the Marseille chefs' weaknesses. He prepares a concentrated aromatic broth of rockfish and adds the whole fish just long enough to cook them so they come away from the bone.

To choose the most refreshing drink with any of the Marseillais fish soups and stews there is no need to look further than the small seaside town of Cassis. It lies in a three-quarter moon valley, 20 kilometres east of Marseille, separated from it by a string of *calanques* which cut into the rocky hills. It's overlooked by Cap Canaille, whose the cliffs are the highest in France.

The first Greek colonists planted vines here. From the 16th to the mid-19th centuries, it was celebrated for its red muscat wines, but now it produces a dry, much sought-after white wine with a characteristic flinty flavour. A handful of compact vineyards are tucked into the crannies around the town, sometimes overlooking the sea, sometimes on terraces carved into the wooded slopes by Cap Canaille.

Collectively, this miniature region may fill no more than 500,000 bottles a year, little enough when measured against the number of *bouillabaisses*, fish soups and grilled fish eaten along the coast each year. In consequence, the wine is not often encountered outside the Midi. The amount of land cultivated, roughly 300 acres, is half of what it was before the Second World War, and it may shrink further because – as elsewhere in the south – real estate tends to be a more profitable investment.

The two best-known vineyards, *Domaine du Paternel* and *Clos Sainte-Magdeleine* make lively wines with bouquets reminiscent of lime trees and cedars. They are meant to be drunk young, and in any case the demand for them is such that you will rarely meet a bottle more than two years old. *Vin de Cassis* should not be confused with the blackcurrant liqueur *Crème de Cassis*, which comes from Burgundy and is best known for its partnership with white wine in the aperitif, named in honour of a past mayor of Dijon, Kir. Those addicted to this aperitif who happen to be passing through Cassis, might try it made with one or other of the local wines.

However picturesque this little port may still be, I cannot help looking over my shoulder and imagining it around 1905 when it was discovered by the painters Matisse, Vlaminck and Derain – *Les Fauves*, 'The wild beasts'. They were captivated by the pink, cream and white houses reflected by the azure water. But it would take more than the glass of *Domaine du Paternel* that I sipped in a waterfront café to blot out the ranks of multi-national motor cruisers that fill the view today.

There may be an element of sour grapes here, because whenever I sit in the port, having cut across country from Marseille, I dream how much more exciting it would be to arrive by boat, after a day spent exploring the *calanques*.

The coastline east of Marseille is pretty. Travel in the other direction and it pays to wait until after dark. I boarded an evening commuter train at the Gare St Charles which shuddered through a string of inner suburbs before emerging at L'Estaque,

Buy Cassis wines at:

Clos Sainte-Magdeleine

AVENUE DE REVESTEL

13260 CASSIS

TELEPHONE 42 01 70 28

or

Domaine du Paternel

CHEMIN DES JANOTS

13260 CASSIS

TELEPHONE 42 01 76 50

a harbour where Marseille's fishing fleet is berthed. Beyond there, the line hugs the bare, rocky coastline, passing the freighters at anchor in the bay below. Then, it starts to dodge through a series of tunnels which leaves passengers playing an involuntary game of peek-a-boo with the full length of Marseille's glittering, twinkling waterfront. The train veers away from the coast at Madrague, creaking to a halt in the villages of Carry-le-Rouet, Sausset-les-Pins and Carro, before skirting the giant BP refinery at Lavera.

The station at Martigues is several kilometres from the town, and – being new to the place – I was fortunate to be given a lift by two catering students. They explained that Martigues was actually three towns or villages (*bourgades*) in one. It's filleted right through the middle by the Coronte canal which links the Mediterranean to the Etang de Berre. On the canal's south bank is the prosperous, modern township of Jonquières and on the north, the dormitory town of Ferrières. Plum in the middle of the waterway is an island village, Brescon, which was called Ile Saint Genest before the French Revolution.

Four hundred years ago, when the three *bourgades* became one town, they united their colours to form a single flag: red for Jonquières, white for the Ile and blue for Ferrières, a standard which ultimately became the *Tricolore* during the Revolution.

I crossed the swing bridge linking Jonquières to the island. Four hundred metres across at its widest point, and split by its own Venetian-style Canal St Sebastien, Brescon has retained a unique quality. On a sharp autumn night, it's dark and silent. One restaurant is open, a couple of cafés, a few small, countrified shops. I booked in at the only *pension* on the island, where the owner Madame Tronc was charming and where the room smelt of blocked drains.

Since the time of Rabelais, Martigues has been celebrated for *poutargue*, dried grey mullet roe, and the first thing I did after unpacking was ask Madame if she could recommend a good source of supply. She knew about *poutargue*, of course she did, but had only bought the hotel a year or so before and was really a foreigner. The shops were closing in five minutes; if I hurried, I might just catch Madame Enoch at the epicerie round the corner.

She was a straight, sturdy grey-haired lady with a husband who wanted to shut

The quiet, island village of Brescon in the middle of Martigues.

up shop and who rattled pots and packages behind an old-fashioned counter. When she was a child the whole of Martigues lived by fishing, she told me. It had less than 10,000 inhabitants. Now it had quadrupled in size and the fishing was a fraction of what it had been. The two big catches were sardines (in summer grilled sardines are still given away to all-comers opposite the Canal St Sebastien) and the grey mullet, the *muge*, which swam from the sea to spawn in the Etang de Berre during the months of July and August.

The fishermen set nets across the mouth of the Canal de Coronte. When they hauled in the catch, they cut out the pair of roes from the females with a small strip of the stomach attached to it so that they dangled like a pair of legs. 'That,' she said, 'is how you can always tell that the *boutargue* comes from Martigues. I have always called it *boutargue* with a b,' she added, 'but most people nowadays say *p-outargue*.

'The women made the *boutargue*,' she told me. 'They salted the roes and flattened them between two stones for a few days before hanging them up to dry in the rafters until they became firm.

'When I was a child fishwives would go through Martigues crying: "*Vingt sous le morceau*", twenty *sous* for a piece. As kids, we didn't have any chocolate. It was our chocolate. We would go up into the loft, break off a bit and eat it, sometimes by itself, sometimes with a piece of bread.'

There was only one fisherman on the island who still made *boutargue*, she sighed; if I was interested in trying some, she would help me. She took me across the road to a paper shop and presented me to the owner. The man's wife was a friend of the woman whose husband caught the *muges*, and she would probably sell me some. Introductions over, I arranged a meeting at nine the next morning.

Madame Ortiz met me at the shop and took me to her flat, a modern block close to the Canal St Sebastien. Her husband was fishing, but she had some *poutargue* for me, wrapped in a sheet of foil. The roe weighed about 200 grams and cost 200 francs, which did not put it into the caviar class, but was not far short of it. It looked like two thin amber slabs of beeswax held together by a small parchment square.

Madame Ortiz cut me a sliver from another piece to sample: it was sweet and salty at the same time. I could imagine how children developed a taste for it, because you could suck it or grate it betweeen your teeth. Nibbling it like this convinced me that it was better to eat *poutargue* like this in its unadulterated state rather than diluted in a paste. I also realized that the restaurant version I had ordered as snack in Orange, pleasant enough in itself, owed nothing to a Martigues mullet.

How had Madame Ortiz's husband, Jean-Claude, come to be the last *muge* man on the Coronte Canal? Once, the fishing rights had belonged to many of the local fishermen who passed them from father to son over generations. As the catch dwindled, many sold their shares to the few who were willing to continue. The canal bank used to be dotted with the mullet-fishers' boat sheds. The Ortiz *cabanon* is a lone survivor on the north shore dwarfed by the massive sweep of a motorway viaduct spanning the canal. Jean-Claude had begun fishing as a boy. He graduated to crew member and finally bought out his uncle's share. His virtual monopoly had earned him a healthy profit, but even this has declined. 'We used to arrive at the end of the year with some nice little savings. Now, I'm afraid, it's hand to mouth.'

Although it is surrounded by heavy industry, I would rather lock myself away on Brescon than in Cassis or any of the other postcard ports. It has no restaurants to excite refined gourmets. The one where I ate, the name escapes me, had a shrivelled waiter in a claret waistcoat who served me an enormous buttery skate wing as part of a 70-franc meal. The island has no medieval quarter, artist's quarter, or even quaint local colour quarter. But it's a thin teardrop of quiet on a much abused coastline.

8

A TASTE OF HONEYED ALMONDS

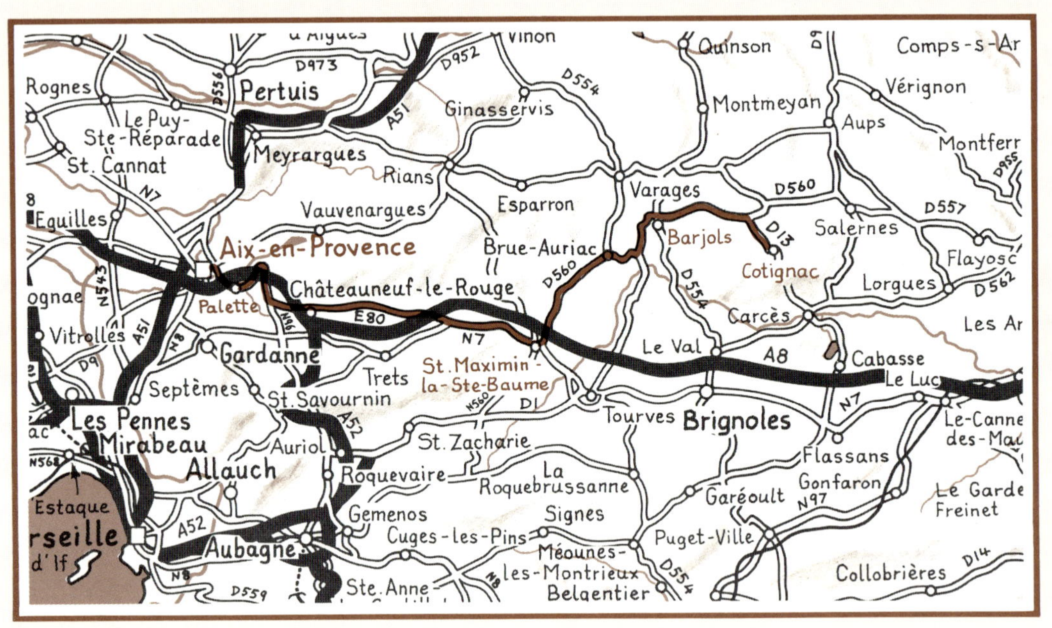

Aix-en-Provence – Palette – St Maximin-la-Ste-Baume – Barjols – Cotignac

A hundred years ago, when the artist, Paul Cézanne lived in Aix-en-Provence, the landscape between Marseille and his home town must have seemed like a vast outdoor laboratory designed by Nature for him to carry out his experiments in light and form. There are still unspoilt areas of rugged countryside, but travelling between the two cities, I felt that their straggling edges had spread towards each other like concrete bindweed until they almost touched.

If the physical gap between them has shrunk, a cultural gulf still distances Aix-en-Provence from its busy neighbour. Aix's Old Town has a chocolate-box feel to it. Even the Cours Mirabeau, an avenue dotted with cafés and divided by two rows of tall designer plane trees is provincially respectable rather than imposing.

There are moments, in the evening, for instance, when the lights go on in the boutique windows, that the network of narrow streets in the old town, looks like a fine piece of cloisonné. It seems almost too pretty to be real. At another time, just after the market closes, when the *clochards* who have been drinking round the bronze boar statue at the bottom end of the Place Richelme start to scavenge, Aix seems almost seedy. Then, in the afternoon before the shops re-open and boys ride skateboards in the square by the Cathédrale St-Sauveur, the streets echo like a playground.

Throughout the Middle Ages, Aix was the nominal capital of Provence, though many of its rulers, kings and dukes of more powerful medieval states either treated it as a playground or exploited it like grasping absentee landlords. Queen Jeanne 'The Beautiful', was a typical Provençal monarch, except that she was a woman. She spent just one year here, in virtual exile from her kingdom of Naples while she faced a charge of murdering her husband. Aquitted, she left immediately.

The one exception was King René who turned the city into a pre-Renaissance centre of arts and culture. Inspired by the Golden Age, he painted, composed motets and wrote poems in the style of the troubadours. In his spare time he kept a flock of 3000 sheep at nearby Gardanne and enjoyed a spot of gardening. Tending vines was his favourite passion. He introduced Neapolitan muscat grapes, and they became the dominant Provençal strain right up to the *phylloxera* epidemic of the last century.

The expansion around its edges, new money, tourism and culture à gogo have brushed a cosmopolitan veneer over modern Aix which masks its underlying Provençal character, but the disguise is done with such style that it's hard to complain. After a bucketful of bitter espressos drunk in village cafes throughout the region, it was a joy to sit at the counter of *Les Rois Mages* in the Rue d'Italie, sipping a demitasse of acidic, freshly-ground Costa Rican coffee, served with a couple of black chocolates; or in another self-indulgent mood to peck at a *tarte caramélisée* – apple tart base, covered in a layer of fluffy, meringue-lightened custard cream with a flat, crusty burnt-sugar roof – from the *Pâtisserie Riederer.*

Les Rois Mages
RUE D'ITALIE
AIX-EN-PROVENCE

Aix's own homespun bonbon is the Calisson, an almond and candied melon lozenge, painted in royal icing. Eating one is like picking the marzipan and icing sugar off a wedding cake, only rather better. It's been made in the Aix for at least 350 years. After the plague in 1630, the priests distributed 'calissouns', blessed by the archbishop, as a specific against the plague. Presumably, the clergy needed to sweeten the population; when Madame de Sévigné visited the town to take the waters in 1672 she commented, 'God is little loved here.'

The candies remained a treat for special occasions until the industrial age, when Aix became the centre of the European almond market. Factories opened to make Calissons. Although most of these have disappeared, the union of Calisson manufacturers still has nine members. The small workshop in the basement of *A La Reine Jeanne*, a confiserie on the Cours Mirabeau employs a workforce of half a dozen, which splits its time between making a lavender honey nougat and Calissons.

A la Reine Jeanne,
32 COURS MIRABEAU
13606 AIX-EN-PROVENCE
TELEPHONE 42 26 02 33

I sympathize with those who find the almond sweets too sickly, but they have a moreish quality. The basic mixture is a paste containing four parts almonds to six parts candied melon and fruit syrup. Considering the quantity of sugar needed to crystallize the melon, it's surprising that is flavour should survive, but it's there as an indefinable fruitiness which mingles with the almond paste.

The process is quite simple. Whole almonds are blanched, chopped and pulped with the fruit. A cook fills the shuttle-shaped die, which has a sheet of rice paper under it, with raw paste, and compacts it – before coating the surface of the calissons with icing. These ready-formed pieces are baked at a low temperature just long enough to set them. Although they keep for about a year, the Aixois believe that they are better in October when the new season's almond crop is used. These were once Provençal almonds, but they now come from all over the Mediterraneaan.

More than 300 tonnes are produced each year by the members of the union and an *appellation d'origine* should mean that all Calissons are equally good. But the choice of almonds may affect the quality, just as the grapes from two adjacent properties may provide widely differing wines. The best Calissons, bought at source and freshly baked, are moister and the aroma of almond more pronounced.

René Jouveau, author of *La Cuisine Provençale de Tradition Populaire*, now in his eighties, cannot remember when Aix ceased to be an important almond centre. As with the olives, he believes, the bottom fell out of the market when they became too expensive to pick.

I met Jouveau by chance. I had dropped into a bookshop to buy a book on Provençal wine-making, a facsimile of an antiquarian tome which, it turned out, cost more than I wanted to pay. The bookseller was friendly, so I asked him to recommend me an authentic Provençal cookery book, from among the dozens which have been published. He sold me Jouveau's book, telling me that the author still lived somewhere in the town.

I took my purchase into the Cathédrale St-Sauveur – churches being a good place for a quiet read in a busy town – and started browsing through it. Written during the 1970s, it evoked a vanishing, poetic Provence, where eating was part of a way of life which had an underlying harmony. Instead of the usual re-hashed recipes for *ratatouille* and *bouillabaisse* which every recipe book seems to produce, there were strange-sounding names: *chouio*, a beefsteak simmered with anchovies and vinegar; *sanguet*, fried chicken's blood with chopped parsley; *gargameu*, a kind of tomato omelette – all dishes of which I had never heard.

Jouveau described a debate on aubergines in which nine worthies vaunted the various ways in which aubergines were prepared in their home-towns. He cited the Nazi collaborator, Charles Maurras' childhood memory of how workers packing dried figs used to place a sprig of statice on each one.

On the spur of the moment, I made up my mind to seek out Monsieur Jouveau. I found his address, an apartment in the Rue Maréchal-Joffre and rang the doorbell.

A woman's head appeared out of a third floor window and invited me up. Madame Jouveau met me at the top of the stairs, greeted me and ushered me into a living room to meet her husband. He was white haired, spectacled, thin. He wore a pair of woolen carpet slippers with the backs trodden down.

M. Jouveau's father had been a friend and colleague of Frédéric Mistral. When Mistral died, Jouveau *père* and René after him took on the responsibility for publishing the *Provençal Almanach*, the chronicle founded by the poet. Mistral and the other members of the 'Félibrige', the school of Romantic poets formed to restore the Provençal language, had written about every aspect of rural life, not least the food. He had named a revue which he published *L'Aïoli*.

René Jouveau felt that the advent of industrially processed and distributed food had led to an inevitable decline in the old ways. He was not a cook himself, but his recipes came directly from people for whom they were part of a way of life. 'The thing that was special,' he said, 'was that every raw material had its own way of being cooked. You did not drop a carrot into a pan and boil it in the same way as beans. Every bean had its own way of cooking.'

Behind many of the so-called specialities there was a purpose, usually of avoiding waste. *Cachat* was one instance. The traditional jam from Apt was not really jam at all, it was a left-over from the candying process. Calissons, presumably were a means of using up scraps of melon. Rice, planted in the Camargue since the Middle Ages, had been a means of desalinating the land. *Mesclun*, the mixed herbs and salad greens, originated from thinnings from the vegetable patch.

'In some of the Vaucluse villages, M. Jouveau explained, 'the butcher's shop opened only for Christmas and Easter, but the relative poverty was balanced by the variety of fruit and vegetables. I came across a seed catalogue published in Marseille in 1854 which offered 28 varieties of fig. Every farmhouse had its fig tree.'

When he was a boy, he had seen Brignoles prunes in Carpentras market, but they no longer existed. The *Cartagène* (fortified wine), made near Nîmes, was not the same, dangerous brew that his father had sampled at Châteauneuf-du-Pape after the Great War.

Perhaps the poetic vision which Jouveau inherited from Mistral never existed,

Vegetable market at Aix-en-Provence.

but something like it must have been there once. Thérèse Plantier, a Provençal writer whose love of Provence is only matched by her loathing of what has happened to it in her lifetime, remembers how the food of the poor peasants she knew during her childhood was one drawn out feast:

> *The wheat, the olives, the adorable kitchen gardens beside streams . . . the pig, the goats, the poultry and rabbits, the surplus of which was sold at the weekly markets, the game, the chub from rivers not yet polluted and full of fish (I used to catch minnows by hand under the stones where they used to flit), and even the crayfish which we poached from the source of the Ouvèze. It was a Land of Cokayne. We ate exquisitely cooked food, 'tians' of marrow or spinach, salt cod with tomato or leeks, little grey snails whose shells coated in cheese we would suck,* soupes au pistou *and haricot beans swimming in fruity oil. (Provence Ma Haine)*

Aix-en-Provence market
daily except Wednesday

La Boulange
RUE RICHELME
AIX-EN-PROVENCE

Latterday Aixois bourgeois probably care as much for their stomachs, but they expect a measure of refinement and class. Butchers and poulterers turn their counter displays into showpieces. Their guinea fowl are wrapped in creamy caul fat. Skinned rabbits are stretched backwards like Russian gymnasts to expose the kidneys. In the *Place Richelme* market, salad sellers behind a mountain of green leaves wait for the clients to buy *mesclun* and *plançons* – young salad leaves picked before full maturity. From the bakers, it is still possible to buy *Pain d'Aix*, a double loaf made in two sections so that one can be eaten fresh and the other a day old with the soup. A cubby-hole of a bread shop, *La Boulange*, towards the top of the Rue Richelme offers a savoury vegetable turnover, a *fouta* – puff pastry filled with a compote of stewed onions and peppers.

Because Aix, a university city, has a cosmopolitan population, its restaurant scene is a melting pot of a dozen nations' cuisines. Tag on the creperies, pizzerias, burger joints and other baited hooks on fast food's greasy line, and it is possible for a careless traveller to miss any trace of local flavour altogether. But there are Provençal restaurants to be found, and the best of them prove that the younger generation of French chefs has the skill and the intelligence to develop the lessons it has learnt.

Jean-Marc Banzo's *Clos de la Violette*, in a residential avenue just outside the central perimeter, looks like a converted suburban house from the outside. Inside, the decoration of the L-shaped room is plain. It certainly lacks the no-expense-spared finish of smart restaurants along the coast. But the cooking has the scent of the *garrigue*. His snail tart has three layers; garlicky snails, sliced and stewed aubergines and crisp herb pastry. It's served with fried parsley sprigs and a fresh tomato sauce. All the main elements: snails, aubergine, tomatoes, herbs and a liberal sprinkling of garlic are part and parcel of the Provençal food baggage. The skill lies in the balancing ingredients, so that they combine to make a whole.

Clos de la Violette
10 AVENUE DE LA VIOLETTE
13100 AIX-EN-PROVENCE
TELEPHONE 42 23 30 71

In Gigondas, I had enjoyed the traditional *pieds et paquets* recipe of stuffed lamb's feet and tripe. At *Clos de la Violette*, the regional concept had been dismantled and put together in as an imaginative variation on a theme. In place of the tripe, M. Banzo had supplied lamb's brains. Instead of using sausage meat, he had stuffed the trotters with garlic so that a gelatinous, garlicky film stuck to the lips with every mouthful. The plate was heavily laden, no tiddler's portion this, and dotted with turnip, potato, carrot, onion and courgettes.

To pretend that the *Clos de la Violette* dish was 'better' than the Gigondas one would be an unfair comparison, but it showed how a clever cook could fuse classic and provincial styles and come up with something new.

As a cheese course, M. Banzo has devized a similar culinary contrast. *La Brousse du Rove* is a goat's cheese made by heating and curdling milk, draining off the whey and eating it, often with sugar like *fromage blanc*, the same day. Into his own smooth home-made *brousse*, he slips three savoury strips of marbling, one of black *tapénade* (an olive and caper paste),one of chopped herbs and a third of red peppers. It's offered with olive-flecked bread, and it's delicious with a glass of the local tipple, *Château Simone*.

René Rougier, who owns the château which makes the wine, is accustomed to hearing his wine discussed with reverence as the Mouton-Rothschild of Provence. I don't rate it that highly, but I still like it very much. Château Simone produces nearly all the wine of the smallest *appellation contrôlée* in France, Palette. It's close to the village of that name on the N7, about eight kilometres from Aix. I took a bus there.

Château Simone

13590 MEYREUIL

TELEPHONE 42 28 92 58

The driver told me: 'You can see Château Simone from the main road, but if you do, you've missed it.'

A twin-turreted, fairy-tale castle, surrounded by a ring of wooded hills, the château is off a side road leading to Meyreuil, and at the end of a track, where a pair of ferocious hounds wait to greet you. The rows of vines laid out neatly on the slopes below it, face north towards Montagne Sainte-Victoire. It's on the site of a monastery, and in the 16th century monks of the order of Grands Carmes d'Aix built the wine cellars as a series of steps into the rock. The present vineyard is much younger – it was started during the last century – but most of the vine-stocks are over fifty years old.

I had drunk the white *Château Simone*, already three years old, with the snail and aubergine tart and also with a langoustine broth. Lighter than a white Châteauneuf du Pape, it's both delicate and spicy. Like all the Rougier wine, it has been aged in oak casks, and it ages better than other white Provençal wines.

The red is kept in beer barrels for three years before bottling. It's vinified from the same grape varieties as Côtes du Rhône – Mourvèdre especially – and, according to René Rougier, is at its best after 20 years. The 1983 vintage had plenty of body, lots of fruit and a complex blend of other aromas.

René Rougier drew my attention to a critique of his rosé which had just appeared in *Cuisine et Vins de France*, which assessed the wine's qualities when drunk with a cauliflower cheese. One 'expert' had commented: 'The wine is astonished, then with sympathetic complacency accepts the dialogue.' The rape of the Sabine women could not be depicted with more tact.

A few kilometres beyond Palette, close to the garlic town of Trets, the N7 crosses the border from Les Bouches du Rhône into the Var. It's a strange, complex *département*, with fascinating contrasts in scenery. Cliffs and gorges dominate its eastern parts, as it grafts on to the Alps; along its Riviera fringe it's neat and manicured. I've always had a soft spot for the comfortable rural swathe of fruit trees, flowers, lavender and vines which runs through the central band. The lemmings scurrying down the Autoroute du Soleil to the beaches ignore it, and it still conceals villages which have not been modernized for rich interlopers.

Making Calissons – Aix's almond-and-melon sweets.

I left the main N7 at St Maximin-la-Ste-Baume on a rainy midweek morning. Heading for Cotignac, I hitched a ride with a retired tax inspector who described with obvious relish a crayfish feast he had enjoyed near there at the Sillans waterfall. He set me down at lunchtime in the sprawling village of Barjols, noted for its *Tripettes*, 'Little Tripe'. An established French guide, *Le Kleber*, once listed these under a Regional Produce of the Var heading as a 'Gastronomic Speciality'. In fact it's not so much a food as a dance which is a highlight of the town's Feast of St Marcel, celebrated in January.

Although it is not a pagan festival, it might well be taken for such. During the plague year of 1349, the neighbouring towns of Aups and Barjols learnt that relics of St Marcel, enshrined in an abandoned monastery near Montmeyan were up for grabs. On the 17th January, the Barjols relic hunters found the monastery gates open, collected the saint's remains and headed for home. On the edge of Barjols, the raiding party met some women washing tripe from an ox which had been slaughtered in commemoration of a bullock which had turned up at an opportune moment to save the inhabitants from famine when the town was being beseiged. The women, it appears jumped for joy when they realized that the town had acquired a saint (which had an important commercial value in the Middle Ages) and started chanting: '*San Maceou, San Maceou, les tripeto vendran leu*' which translates approximately as St Marcel gets the tripe.

Off and on since then, the Barjolais have celebrated the relic's arrival by killing an ox, roasting it and dancing a jig which they call *la tripette*. The fact that Marcel's remains, barring a finger, were calcinated when the church was set alight during the Wars of Religion in the 16th century has not deterred them.

In recent years, the celebrations have enjoyed a Clochemerlesque reputation. One bullock nearly died during the procession. It had been bought in Marseille and the mayor decked the beast in a coat on which had been printed 'I'm going to be roasted.' The poor creature was then marched to Barjols. On the way, it fell sick and could barely stand during the procession. It was touch and go whether it would get to the slaughterhouse. During its trans-Provençal hike it contaminated a cow, which died. Since then the ox is accompanied by a veterinary certificate.

The old spit on which the beef was roasted was turned by muscle power and free rations of plonk. In 1939, there was an argument as to whether the spit's owner had the right to charge for its loan and a mechanically turned spit replaced it. However, on one occasion the Mistral blew and instead of being roasted, the beast was carbonized, so that in recent years the ox roast has been faked, while the cut-up real ox is being spit roasted elsewhere.

Animal rights groups have complained, and the French bureaucracy has intervened. An inspector from Draguignan refused to permit the organizers to slay the ox on the grounds that they were advertising sacred beef for sale without paying the appropriate taxes. The organizers found a way round the ban by giving away the beef and selling the paper in which it was wrapped.

From an electrician, who gave me a ride out of the town, I learnt how to trip the Tripettes. It takes place in the main square, the Place de la Rouguière, when the live ox is paraded there, and again when the carcass was being fitted on to the spit. As he described it, it seemed more of a wild bounce than a measured step, in time to the *galoubets* and *tambourins*, pipes and drums made especially in the village. Everybody from officials, cooks and the ox's bodyguard to spectators joins in.

I had to walk the last few kilometres into Cotignac through a downpour. It's probably the best way of seeing this strange village for the first time. The *route départmentale* emerges from a gently rolling landscape of woods and vines, zig-zags sharply and emerges on top of a sheer cliff with the straggling streets of the village tucked close under its face. On foot, it's possible to trace a route down through a series of lanes to one side of the cliff and then, looking back and up at it, you can see that it has been pitted with abandoned cave dwellings scooped into the rock-like holes in a cheese.

Having booked a room for the night and changed into some dry clothes, I found the first available café, sat down at a table with a dark brown poodle sitting in the chair opposite and ordered some coffee. A heated political discussion was underway at the next table orchestrated by one of Jean-Marie Le Pen's Front National supporters. 'The rotten democracy we have today,' he argued, large, fat and slapping his hand on the marble top to enforce his point, 'is worse than a dictatorship.'

In the wine cellar at Château Simone.

Yves Guieu's beehives: they produce some of the best honey in the world.

After dark, when the rain had stopped, I crossed the village high street, avoided a restaurant advertising *foie gras* and caviar *together*, and dropped into a small *pension, Lou Calen*. As I drank red wine from the Cotignac co-operative, I read the village's own newspaper, *La Semaine*. Page two carried the banner headline: 'Death of an Olive Tree, Victim of Man's Folly.'

'Yes!' the story read, 'an olive tree has succumbed. But what, you may ask, is one tree less? Nothing, almost nothing. STOP! An olive tree is precious. That we should be obliged to sacrifice those suffering from disease or those destined to warm mankind fair enough. But for pity's sake, Mr Driver, slow down so that none may die! Neither you nor the trees. This, however, was the fate of one of these trees, symbols of Provence. A car speeding between Carcès and Montfort, left the road and crashed. Under the violence of the impact an olive tree at the side of the road was uprooted and broken in half!'

The sheer, grisly horror of the piece nearly ruined my appetite. The main dish was a *Civet de Sanglier*, real boar, well-hung, gamey, marinated and the sauce thickened with blood. It was strong-tasting, and good – but a shock to a digestive system weaned on tamed food.

Les Ruchers du Bessillon
83850 COTIGNAC
TELEPHONE 94 04 60 39

My main reason for passing through Cotignac was to search for something less assertive than the boar stew. I wanted to try its honey. *Les Ruchers du Bessillon* is to honey what Chanel No. 5 is to scent. The comparison is not so far fetched, since honey aromas are, to me, every bit as subtle as perfume or wine. Yves Guieu runs the family business from an old-fashioned store. The back wall is lined with metal drums labelled with the many varieties he sells: chestnut, lavender, acacia, pine, lime, heather, thyme, sunflowers and rosemary. Each type has its own style, its own texture, its own special aroma.

The family business has kept hives for over a century. M. Guieu thinks that he owns about 800. He moves them around Provence and as far as the Jura to wherever the flowers are. Hives are located so that the bees will naturally forage from the appropriate nectar. Grazing rights are normally paid to the owners of the land in kind; they receive honey for every hive. This is more of a token, since the bees are essential to the flowers' pollination. Acacia gives a pale runny honey. Chestnut honey is reminiscent of *crème de marrons.* Lavender honey is pale and tallowy, but has a lingering taste of perfumed wild flowers. Rosemary honey has an almond-paste texture and a sweet fruity scent. The lime honey, starting to crystallize, was stronger and velvety.

It occurs to me that those descriptions do not reflect how the individual honeys might be at another time of year. When freshly extracted from the hive and bottled it might be smooth and liquid and taste quite different. An opaque 'millefleurs' in autumn might have been a translucent 'millefleurs' in spring. Honey is alive and from the runny stage it will always eventually crystallize.

Monsieur Guieu thought that the only contribution he made to the individual characteristics of his products was in the way he looked after the hives. When, for instance he moved them from the Grand Plan de Canjure above Aups where, for argument's sake, they may have been set in lavender fields, he would clean them out before resiting them among the chestnut woods around Collobrières. That way there was no risk of the honey garnered from one source of nectar blending with another and blurring the flavour. I can understand why visitors to Provence rave about its honey-flavoured Calissons and nougat, but I can't think of a better way of eating honey than straight out of a jar, with a spoon.

9

ROSÉS AND RED BANDOL

Brignoles – Les Arcs – Toulon – Le Pradet – Cap de Carqueiranne – Bandol – Ollioules – Le Beausset – St Tropez – Cogolin

Despite its name, Côtes de Provence is an *appellation contrôlée* which is limited almost exclusively to the *département* of the Var. It cuts a thick swathe through the hinterland from the outskirts of Toulon to the slopes above Draguignan down to the coast at St Raphael, while a second band between the Massif des Maures and the sea stretches to the cultural carbuncle of St Tropez.

The administrative centre for the *appellation* and the place where many of the best wines in this disparate region are produced is Les Arcs. To get there from Cotignac, I first bused my way back to the N7 at Brignoles, staying there just long enough to discover that the plum trees which produced the famous Brignoles prunes had been cut down in the 16th century during fighting between religious factions. Only the name remained and, according to the lady at the tourist office, any plum dried in the Var might be labelled as coming from her town.

Something like two-thirds of all wines made inside the Côtes de Provence limits is rosé. Along the N7, hoardings every few hundred metres advertise vineyards or mass-produced brands. Tracking down the best producers or even good ones can be something of a hit and miss experience, because rosé wines, among the easiest to make, are probably the hardest to make successfully.

Just what is vin rosé? Some people assume that it is a blend of red and white wines, but it isn't. It is vinified with red grapes: in Provence, Grenache, Cinsault, Mourvèdre and Syrah. Rosé can be vinified as an 'off-red' *or* an 'off-white' wine.

In the first case, the process is known as *saignée* which means bleeding. The *vendange* takes place just before the grapes reach full maturity. They are crushed and mixed up rather than pressed, and the clear juice goes into the vat along with the purple skins which dye the juice. Fermentation starts and as soon as the nascent wine attains the desired colour, it is siphoned into a second vat to finish fermenting.

The second kind of rosé is more of a phoney white. It's still made from the same red grapes, but the pressing stage is more vigorous, so that the juice becomes slightly coloured by the skins. The juice only (not the skins) goes into the vat and fermentation takes place. This gives a paler rosé (sometimes called a *gris*, that is grey wine), but one with less tannin.

Sample and buy regional wines at:

Maison des Vins de Côtes de Provence

SYNDICAT DES VINS COTES DE PROVENCE
83460 LES ARCS-SUR-ARGENS
TELEPHONE 94 73 31 01

Rosés de Provence

Names to watch out for:

Château Real Martin (Le Val)
Château Grand'Boise (Trets)
Château Minuty (Gassin)
Château de Roux (Giraud)
Château de Barbeyrolles (Gassin)
Domaine de l'Abbaye (Le Thoronet)
Domaine de la Croix (La Croix Valmer)
Domaine de Curebasse (Fréjus)
Domaine des Planes (Roquebrune-sur-Argens)
Domaine de Malherbe (Bormes-les-Mimosas)
Domaine Bastide des Bertrands (Cannet-des-Maures)

The best local vineyards are:

Commanderie de Peyrassol
FLASSANS-SUR-ISSOLE
83340 LE LUC
TELEPHONE 94 69 71 02

Domaine de la Bernarde
off the N7
83340 LE LUC
TELEPHONE 94 60 71 31

Domaine des Féraud
on the D48
83550 VIDAUBAN
TELEPHONE 94 73 03 12

Château Sainte-Roseline
just off the N555
83460 LES ARCS-SUR-ARGENS
TELEPHONE 94 73 32 75

Domaine des Hauts de St Jean
83460 LES ARCS-SUR-ARGENS
TELEPHONE 94 73 31 09

Off the main road between Brignoles and Les Arcs are three of the most accomplished wine-makers north of the Massif des Maures: *Commanderie de Peyrassol* at Flassans-sur-Issole; *Domaine de la Bernarde* at Le Luc and *Domaine des Féraud* outside Vidauban. All three wines can be sampled at the *Maison des Vins de Côtes de Provence*, an elegant villa on the outskirts of Les Arcs, which acts as a showroom and shop for the best in the region. It's an ideal place to go for anybody about to spend a holiday in southern Provence. Here you can quickly and simply find which producers to trust and how much to pay for a bottle. That way restaurant rip-offs and nasty wines in pretty bottles can be avoided.

Les Arcs is the home of Baron Rasque de Laval, President of the *Grand Ordre de Méduse*, the professional body which promotes all the southern Provençal wines. His property, Château Ste-Roseline, a Romano-Gothic abbey, contains the saint's relics and a 110-year-old Carignan vine classified as a historic monument. He produces one of the few great Côtes de Provence red wines (although *Domaine de la Bernarde* is arguably *the* best).

I was more curious about rosés than reds, so I preferred to drop in on Henri Pawloski. This ex-truck-driver studied the vigneron's craft in the agricultural college at Toulon-Hyères. His property, Domaine des Hauts de St Jean, is just outside the village, but the work of vinification goes on in a hangar behind the parish church in the centre of Les Arcs.

He belongs to the increasing number of young professionals who are helping to resurrect the reputation of Côtes de Provence by employing precise techniques, flair and no little love for their work. Their main advantage over previous generations is that they can control heat. The Mediterranean sun which befriends the grower was often an enemy to the wine maker who could not control the fermentation temperatures crucial to a successful vintage. Modern vats can be thermostatically controlled to prevent the fermenting juice from overheating.

Rosés were once described as *vin d'une nuit*, one night wine, a reference to the length of time the juice and skins lay together in the vat before the liquid was drawn off. That gives a clue as to the constraints under which they were made, and the variations to which they must have been subject.

Nobody needs to be an expert to appreciate the qualities which make a good rosé. It should be clear and bright; a pale wine will taste as weak and drab as it appears; the shade of pink may vary, but if it is too dark, the wine may be more tannic; if orange, oxydized.

Henri Pawloski produces several rosés. Each year he experiments with new blends or single varietal ones. Some are based on Grenache, some on Mourvèdre. All have a brilliant sparkle and intense salmon-pink colour. The one he let me taste last was unique; vinified from Syrah grapes it had an irresistible after-taste of strawberries and raspberries.

Just as Côtes du Rhône subdivides into smaller distinct zones such as Vacqueyras and Gigondas, Côtes de Provence has a small, affiliated, but separate *appellation*, Bandol. To visit Bandol meant catching a train back to the coast at Toulon, the naval port squatting under the limestone massif of Mont Faron. Late on a November evening when I arrived, with a cold Mistral whipping across the Quai de la Sinse, it wasn't the place for a leisurely walkabout.

One of the restaurants on the quay, *Herrero*, did its best to show me the disdain it felt for casual customers, serving up a *salade chaude* of overstewed fish anointed with cheap oil, an octopus *daube* with a dark and acid sauce and a tired, granular lemon tart which would have seemed bad even in a motorway cafeteria.

I left feeling glad that I had not ordered *bourride*. Toulon's best known speciality is a white-fish stew. Like *bouillabaisse* it has a '*Charte*' to which upwards of thirty restaurants including *Herrero* are affiliated. It seemed to me at the time to have about as much credibility as a baked bean charter, because it puts no emphasis on the cook's skill or the fishes' freshness. But the Mistral is notorious for making people bad tempered, and I may have been responding to its influence.

Next morning the gale was still blowing. I felt duty bound to give the city and its fish a second chance. On the strength of its name and location I decided to look up a fish restaurant, *L'Oursinado* (the word describes a dish of white fish in a sauce thickened with a purée of sea urchins) at Cap de Carqueiranne. A bus ride to Le Pradet and a bracing walk found me at a roundabout in a wood of parasol pines, olive trees and Arbutus bushes whose prickly fruit lay dotted over the ground.

L'Oursinado

NEAR LES OURSINIERES

83220 LE PRADET

TELEPHONE 94 21 77 06

(Closed from November to end of February)

L'Oursinado, at the end of a rough track, did not look as though it was doing much business. In fact, the whole of its front had been ripped off and a couple of men were laying new foundations. One was Daniel Finimondi, the owner, the other his chef. They were carrying out a quiet refurbishment, during the four winter months that they closed the restaurant. Perhaps, I should have felt cheated of my lunch, but I was glad of the chance to talk to the patron off-duty.

His restaurant only barbecued fish on a large, sooty outdoor grill. What he sold depended on what he could buy from his contacts. He only bought Mediterranean fish: 'I went to the Caribbean four years ago,' he recalled, 'Guadeloupe, St Martin, Martinique, and I bought fish off the boats in the mornings, still flapping in the boxes, but they were tasteless by comparison with what I buy here.' He preferred dorade, sar and the other better tasting members of the bream family.

There was no menu as such. He sold whatever he had by the gutted weight. 'The price of fish is elastic,' he claimed. 'Last year, I had a bream weighing $1\frac{1}{2}$ kilos, but by the time I had removed the tripe it was half that weight.' Except for the mullet which he left untouched, he gutted and scraped the fish, brushed them with a mixture of oil, lemon juice, thyme and rosemary and slapped them on to a grill on which he burnt fennel stalks. In summer *L'Oursinado* can be full of holidaying families, packed like sardines. And Daniel admitted that some of them might receive, if not a raw then a slightly overcooked deal.

L'Oursinado is on a mole overlooking the Gulf of Giens. We climbed down onto the rocks below the terrace where the waves spilled over into the rock pools and the crannies filled with wind-blown foam. The restaurant had taken its name from the sea urchin beds which were once abundant on this stretch of the coast. When he was younger, Daniel collected the spiny balls here as easily as kids pick conkers, pierced the shells and scooped out the stars of orange roe. 'Nobody used to pay for them then,' he said. 'Now, they are worth their weight in gold.'

Bandol is the other side of Toulon, so I bused back to the city-centre and headed off in the other direction, past the industrial and residential estates of La Seyne, through Six-Fours-Les-Plages and Sanary-sur-Mer.

The small resort was, if it's possible to say this of a whole community, hungover

See urchins, once plentiful along the coast, are disappearing.

You can buy Bandol wines at:

Domaines du Bandol

MAISON DES VINS DE BANDOL
ALLEE VIVIEN
83150 BANDOL
TELEPHONE 94 29 45 03

Bandol

Names to watch out for:

Domaine Tempier
Domaine Pibarnon
Château Ste-Anne
La Bastide Blanche

plus, of course,

Domaine de Terrebrune

GEORGES DELILLE
83190 OLLIOULES
TELEPHONE 94 74 01 30

from its annual wine fair. Many of the hotels were closed and the Auberge du Port, where the local wine producers entertain clients, was resting. Although the town has given its name to the best known of the coastal wines, the vineyards themselves lie snug in the hills and hollows behind it, some stretching back almost into Toulon.

A taxi left me at an inn on the road to Le Beausset. My luck had temporarily run out, because the modest dinner at the *Auberge des Pins* was relieved only by a bottle of *Domaine de Terrebrune*. It was a politic choice, since I had arranged to meet Georges Delille, the grower, next day.

In general terms, Bandol wines are big, round and tannic, containing at least 50 per cent Mourvèdre grapes. They may need a couple of years in barrels followed by ten years in the bottle before they reach their prime. Although the Phocians planted vines here 2000 years ago, the modern *appellation contrôlée* is only 50 years old.

The *Domaine de Terrebrune* is an impeccable vineyard spread across a broad valley within sight of the sea. It's one of the youngest members of the Bandol family. Monsieur Delille abandoned his business selling luxury French table-settings to buy the property. Starting from scratch, he bulldozed the land, planted the vines, built the cellars and has dedicated himself to his vocation with a sense of idealism verging on the obsessive.

What makes a good winegrower? It must be attention to little details or rather, the refusal to cut corners. A vine has two parts; its root stock and the grafted vine which grows from it and which supplies the grape variety from which the wine is eventually made. The farming of a vineyard involves pruning, weeding (without the use of herbicides for all quality wines including M. Delille's), protecting the stock against the rigours of winter, controlling the setting and harvesting at precisely the right moment.

Every July, when the grapes change colour, M. Delille has to decide which surplus bunches to cut away. As a rule he will leave only one bunch to ripen per shoot of new growth; it reduces the amount of wine he can make, but should produce a grape with more sugar, which in turn will provide a wine with more alcohol.

One of M. Delille's sidelines is designing expensive crystal wine glasses. They have narrow rims which dip and swell outwards like a once-trim man who has thickened at the waist. It's a shape which allows a taster to swirl the wine in the glass without slopping it over the tablecloth. Aerating a Bandol is a bit like giving Sleeping Beauty a kiss; it wakes the old dear up. Old is perhaps an operative word, because the wine in its prime is at least ten years old. Then it's velvety, the tannins softened and the bouquet of violets discreet.

We set about tasting a decade of Bandol vintages. A friend of the family was installing a computerized stock-control system in the office next door. He emerged to join us in the small bar. Madame arrived circa 1984, and was gently teased for not recognizing the year. About 1981 a van called to collect a few cases of Bandol rosé, and the driver shared a glass with us. In 1978, or maybe it was 1976, we decided to go out for lunch.

La Nonna is set back from the road in a rough patch of Mediterranean savanna between Ollioules and Le Beausset. It does not have so much as a sign outside to show that it's a restaurant, and looks for all the world like a modern, residential *pavillon*. Madame Delille objected to the striped Regency wallpaper, as any bourgeoise of taste would, but she tucked into the food. The stuffed mussels from Bouzigues, plump with just enough breadcrumbs to mop up the oil and butter were a pretext for trying a white Bandol from the *Château Sainte-Anne*.

Auberge de la Nonna
QUARTIER DE LA REPPE
83330 LE BEAUSSET
TELEPHONE 94 90 36 06

The main dish was a *daube de boeuf*, beef stew, which led to a little incident that throws a light on how Provençal cooks cook. It was beautifully aromatic, tasting of sage, thyme, dried orange peel and red wine all carefully dosed. 'La Nonna' herself, Madame Sauze, ventured from her kitchen to ask whether we had enjoyed it. We cooed and beamed our appreciation, and I showed off a bit by complimenting her on the juniper berries in the sauce. Her response was a mixture of shock, surprise and a hint of anger with her assistant in the kitchen.

She had owned a bistro in Marseille for 20 years before coming to Ollioules, and she had been cooking all her life. When *she* cooked a *daube*, she always made sure that the different flavours blended into each other so that it was impossible to pick out the ingredients one from another. Although we insisted on how much we enjoyed her *daube*, she felt she had let us down. The first thing she did after clearing our plates was to go into the kitchen, taste the sauce and return to apologize.

The taste of local lemons flavours fish dishes and salads.

The pick of the crop. It's taken for granted that salad ingredients are perfect.

Foreigners may assume, rightly nine times out of ten, that rustic food is about robust, uncomplicated flavours, the zing of orange zests, the attack of garlic, the fragrance of wild herbs. It comes as a shock to realize that the genuine cooks think so hard about the simple dishes which they simmer on the side of their stoves. The story goes, it may be apocryphal but it makes sense, that in the old days when *daubes* were cooked over an open fire, the pans they were cooked in were never cleaned. A crust of dried sauce finished by lining the inside of the pan and it was this which gave *daubes* their special flavour.

Madame Sauze also insisted on the fact that she made her own *anchoïade*. To Provençals, it is an essential seasoning and its discreet presence is the secret ingredient in many dishes, the one element they accidentally on purpose forget to mention when they give you a recipe. It's basically a paste made by anchovies, olive-oil and garlic passed through a mouli-légumes, but some cooks may add a dash of vinegar and almost all will flavour their *anchoïade* with basil or thyme.

A coach service connects Toulon with St Tropez. Its route passes through the coastal band of Côtes-de-Provence, where vineyards rival those from the other side of the Massif des Maures. One, and an outstanding one too, *Domaine Ott* at La Londe-les-Maures, produces a white wine, *Clos Mireille*, described by a French critic as 'Without doubt one of the poorest values for money in France'. The Ott family can afford to cock a snook at comments like this, since an inflated price has never prevented the world's most famous restaurants from buying what it produces.

Several of the best bargains come from vineyards either in or close to the St Tropez Peninsula: *Château de Barbeyrolles* (which makes a lovely, pale rose-petal rosé) and *Château Minuty*, both near Gassin and *Domaine de la Tourraque* at Ramatuelle.

Even in late autumn, when the tornado of vulgarity which devastates this small town every year has blown over, St Trop. is an ungainly place. Most of the day, the D98 which branches off the main road is choked with crawling cars and trucks negotiating the roadworks set up to repair the summer damage. In winter, when the hordes of tourists have gone, many of the boutiques and trendy cafés shut. Then the most animated spots are the Jean-Reveille Mole where the older inhabitants sit and swap gossip or the Place Les Lices where men play boules.

Many rich and famous stars still own or buy expensive hideaways, order elegant dinners from *Le Chabichou* or disappear into the sunset on glitzy yachts, but they are an elusive breed which does not enjoy rubbing shoulders with the crowds in front of the *Café Senequier*. They would never be seen preening themselves on the *Plage de la Bouillabaisse*. Even the fading star, Brigitte Bardot who helped to invent the St Trop. myth has announced that she is selling her home and moving out.

Micka
9 RUE LOUIS-LEBLANC
83990 ST TROPEZ

St Tropez does have a deliciously unsophisticated local speciality. Away from the old town in the Rue Louis-Leblanc is a perfectly ordinary boulangerie-patisserie which sells the extraordinary *tarte tropézienne*. It was created by a Polish baker Alexandre Micka who patented it in 1971, before selling the small chain of bakeries he owned along the coast. It's a soft, bun-like brioche. The recipe must be similar to the ancient Sally Lunn, filled with a lightened custard cream. It's coated in crystallized sugar to give it a crunchy surface. I bought two large slices and gollopped them one after the other. The *tarte*'s charm lies in it being a kind of nursery pudding. Eaten with a fork it would be pleasant. But for the full effect it's best grasped and bitten into; the custard squeezes out of the sides like toothpaste from a wounded tube, and either slops on the floor or splurges a creamy tidemark around the eater's mouth. It's impossible to swallow a *tarte tropézienne* without licking the lips afterwards.

The St Tropez Peninsula has some of the most expensive real estate in France. The pitch used by agents is that if the prices go through the roof, only the rich will want to live here and the town will revert to being the classy playground it once was. Unfortunately, the cafés, bistros and restaurants all apply the same principle without providing equivalent value on the plate. Nor in the bottle. A *Château Minuty* rosé which costs less than 50 francs from the property may sell for five times that amount in some unscrupulous eateries.

To give some impression of the totally artificial state which exists, St Tropez has less than 6000 inhabitants, yet the French food guide *Gault et Millau* manages to say a kind word for about 20 restaurants, and they represent just a small proportion of what is on offer. What seems to me so sad is that skilled chefs go to endless pains concocting 'regional' dishes of scampi with cream and chive sauce, for instance, when

La Ferme du Magnan
off the N98
83310 COGOLIN
TELEPHONE 94 49 57 54
(Weekends only in winter)

the cream probably comes from Normandy and the frozen scampi tails all the way from the west coast of Scotland.

La Ferme du Magnan, part farm, part restaurant is near Cogolin, off the main Hyères road, about ten kilometres from St Tropez. It's the ideal place to escape to after a dose of the Riviera blues; a long, low cottage with its back against a hillside dotted with olives and cork oaks. On the terrace in front of the farm stands the twisted trunk of an ancient mulberry tree. To one side a stack of old vine stocks are piled to the height of the roof. Chicken, guinea fowl and ducks criss-cross the gravel track winding up to the farm. 'Magnan' means silk worm. Generations ago, the farms around Cogolin used to supply the raw material for a flourishing local silk industry. Those days are gone.

Claude Campanile rears poultry; his wife, Brigitte, cooks it. He was born on a farm near Cogolin. She grew up in the country, but outside Paris. *La Ferme du Magnan* celebrates the kind of food with which Claude grew up: 'I saw the Provençal way of life disappearing and I wanted to do something to preserve it.'

What he has idealized are the recipes which women cooked to please their men. 'Brigitte,' he explained, 'learnt the specialities of my mother and my aunts who were all good cooks.' Their role was not so much subservient as the consequence of a natural division of labour. If filling a plate with food was their duty, giving it a special savour was an act of love. It's the underlying difference between the chef in love with his 'Art' and the dedicated home cook.

The Campaniles have mirrored the old relationship in their restaurant. Claude looks after the chicken house. Some are kept in pens; others roam at will. He slaughters them himself in a small approved abattoir and uses a plucking machine with rubber flails to remove the feathers. In the restaurant, he doubles as waiter and wine steward. Brigitte does the cooking, most of it on a grill fuelled by the old vines, in a large open chimney-piece. The vine wood gives a taste which is both smoky and reminiscent of wine to the split hens, mussels and tripe sausages which are part grilled, part roasted over the embers.

Her short menu includes guinea fowl simmered in Bandol, Barbary duck with olives, a young farmyard cock stewed with morells, a chicken liver pâté and the *soupe*

At La Ferme du Magnan – *just 10 km from St Tropez, but in another world.*

au pistou. René Jouveau, whom I'd met in Aix, believed that this soup originated in Marseille, because Marseillais used to keep pots of basil in their windows like Florentines during the hot summer months. But it is so obviously a simple vegetable soup, that it defies any savant's research into its origins. The '*pistou*' part of it, is a Provençal adaptation of the Ligurian '*pesto*', made by pounding basil leaves in a mortar. Smaller spiky-leaved basil, pulled up by the roots tends to have a stronger flavour than the floppy broad-leaved basil which is usually grown under glass in cooler climes.

In the peak of the season, *La Ferme du Magnan* is normally packed full – with local residents rather than the holidaymakers who throng the beaches of St Tropez. Without the traffic, it would be a 15-minute drive from the coast. But the bumper-to-bumper ride could take up to an hour and a half. On this out-of-season weekday, I was the only visitor, and the sense of peace was complete.

In winter the *Ferme du Magnan* only opens at the weekends so Brigitte and Claude shared a scratch lunch with me around their kitchen table. We ate slices of a *caillette du Massif des Maures*, a dark, herby meatloaf. Claude had extracted the recipe from a retiring charcutier in Cogolin. While we were tucking in, Brigitte prepared an impromptu salad of lettuces and tomatoes, turning it and turning it in a dressing of salt, lemon juice and a generous dose of oil.

There are four typical French Mediterranean salads. *Salade niçoise* is a mixed salad with beans, eggs, potatoes and anchovies added to the normal mixed salad ingredients. *Mesclun* is a blend of salad greens and herbs, maybe a dozen varieties, sown together and picked immature to provide textures from gossamer fine to crunchy and shades of taste from bitter to sweet. The typical winter salad combines curly endive with *chapons* of fried bread rubbed with garlic. But the best salads are the ones which *happen.* It's taken for granted that the ingredients are perfect. If baby artichokes are in season, fine; if it's corn salad, known as *doucette* (little soft one) in the Midi, well and good; or maybe it's tender young white-stemmed, wild dandelion leaves with their faint taste of aloes.

Remembering the old days, Claude pointed through the kitchen window across to the hills on the other side of the valley. When he was a child, he told me, he used to go there with his father to burn charcoal. They used to stay out all night, because the baking wood needed careful watching or it would catch alight. For a dare he would climb on top of the mound, knowing that if it had been badly constructed, it might collapse under him. They would bring back wild mushrooms with them, too, especially the fleshy *sanguines*. Nobody burnt charcoal now; the craft had died out. He asked me whether I had noticed a flock of sheep on the way out. It belonged, he explained, to the last shepherd in the commune.

10

HAUTE CUISINE PROVENÇALE

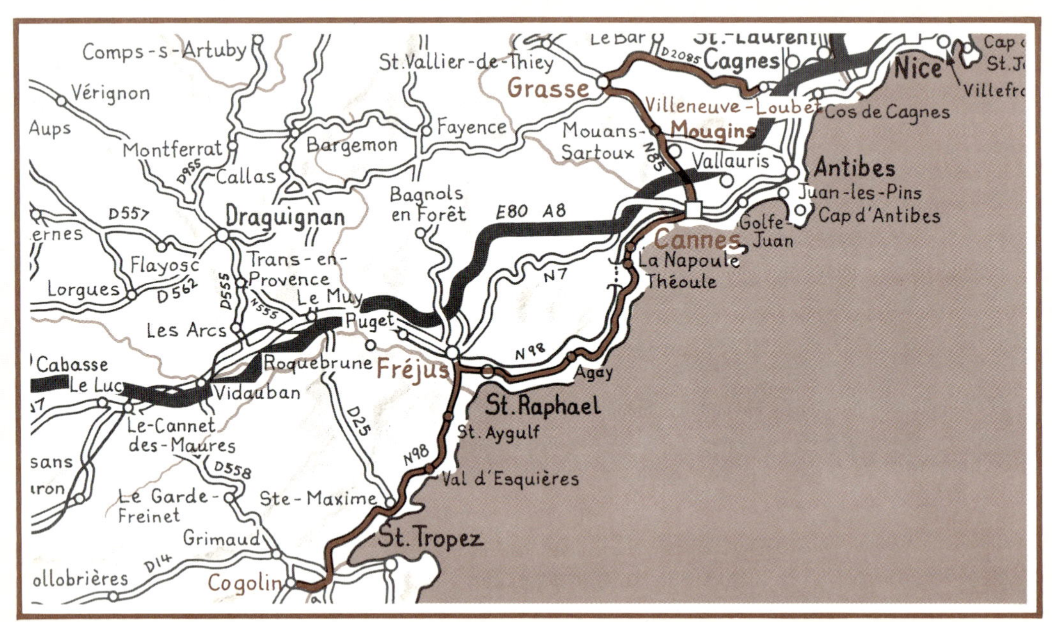

Cogolin – Fréjus – Cannes – Mougins – Grasse – Villeneuve-Loubet

In Cogolin, where I spent the night, is a small museum dedicated to Raimu, the actor who starred in many of Marcel Pagnol's movies. His roles as a melancholic baker in *La Femme du Boulanger* and César the Marseillais café owner in *Marius* ensured that they became classics of French cinema history. Housed upstairs in an anonymous looking building in a dead end somewhere near a school, the museum has just the right degree of quirkiness to appeal to a film buff. Two prize relics, the baker's bread box and César's trousers are displayed in places of honour.

I don't think it's an accident that Provence's two best-loved mythical characters provided the community with bread and wine. Food and drink have been saving graces in a country which has been torn apart throughout its history by piously motivated massacres, corrupt politics and brigandage. To Pagnol, a free-thinker, they symbolized a solid value which Raimu with his bull's neck and ample girth exemplified to perfection.

The coastal road I took from Cogolin to Fréjus passes through the resorts of Port Grimaud, Ste Maxime, Val d'Esquières and St Aygulf. It was December, and they were in a state of hibernation. Without the colour and movement of people to vitalize them, the shuttered roadside cafés, bars and *'restaurants gastronomiques'* appeared dusty and drab. It's tempting to see the French Riviera as one extended waterside city, made up of suburbs, each with its own status and character. This stretch is the least glamorous.

At Fréjus, I boarded a train which chuntered round the Esterel Corniche, along the gulf of La Napoule and into Cannes. The popular image of the Film-Festival town is usually restricted to the curving length of the Croisette and Le Suquet, the old quarter. But the town has a population of 100,000 for whom the Film Festival every May is no more than a minor distraction. Buying tomatoes in the market at Forville or finding a parking space on a Monday morning are, rightly, of more concern to them.

If a prize were awarded to the inhabitants of the Côte d'Azur who cared most for their stomachs, those living in Cannes and particularly in the neighbouring village of Mougins would deserve any culinary Palme d'Or.

Cristal
13–15 ROND-POINT DUBOYS D'ANGERS
06400 CANNES
TELEPHONE 93 39 45 45

Royal Gray
6 RUE DES ETATS-UNIS
06400 CANNES
TELEPHONE 93 99 04 59

The town does have its fantasy side. The head-waiter at the Lebanese-owned hotel *Cristal* (which is billed curiously as 'almost luxurious') looks as though he has stepped off the set at Dynasty's La Mirage. He managed to find time, going up in the lift to the restaurant on the top floor, to tell me that he was from Bordeaux and that I would do better to try his restaurant's food in six months' time. Whether the chef was having an off day or whether the hotel had employed an incompetent one, he did not make clear. The six months is up.

I found luxury for real at the *Gray d'Albion*, the *Royal Gray*'s restaurant. Here Jacques Chibois has managed to bring warmth and character to another, less prepossessing Lebanese hotel. Although he was only 26 when he joined the hotel as its executive chef in 1981, the management gave Chef Chibois *carte blanche* to implement his own plans. 'First of all,' he outlined, 'I opened the *Royal Gray*, a gastronomic restaurant, because I had noticed that Cannes lacked a prestige restaurant. The hotel was suffering from a double handicap – it was modern, and off the Croisette – and needed an outstanding feature to attract outside customers.'

It took him eight years before *Gault et Millau* voted the *Royal Gray* its restaurant of the year. Serving 120 covers a day, it earns the hotel over 10,000,000 francs a year. This is only a fraction of the small catering empire which Chef Chibois manages within the hotel. That empire includes a discotheque, a brasserie, a beach restaurant, a Lebanese restaurant, banqueting, room service and a staff cafeteria. While the stars and starlets are working their way through his *Croustillant de thon tiède* (warm fresh tuna), or *Loup 'nouvelle vague' a l'huile vierge et à la vanille* (vanilla flavoured sea-bass in olive-oil) computers in the hotel's guts are checking that the cumulative ratio of raw materials to sales never drifts beyond their 30 per cent target.

Where money is no object, it is easy to spend 1000 francs at the *Royal Gray*, especially if one's taste is for raviolis garnished with caviar. But extravagance is not essential. At midday there is a 'bargain' *prix fixe* menu, which may not have *foie gras* on it, but where the cooking of hake with turnips or puff-pastry with sautéed apples and caramel sauce or sea-bream with baby onions and olive-oil are quite affordable *chefs d'oeuvre*.

Jacques Chibois epitomizes the new generation of chefs. He took an agricultural degree before turning to professional cookery, and learnt the ropes by working in a string of three-star kitchens. He admired Michel Guérard, one of Nouvelle Cuisine's prime movers, for his imagination, his finesse and 'his willingness to trust youngsters by giving them responsibility'. From Jean Delaveyne, Guérard's own mentor, he learnt a horror of the self-deluding mental blindness which pushes cooks into denaturing food through an exaggerated sense of aesthetics. Louis Outhier at *La Napoule*, who built up a three-star restaurant from a simple *pension*, taught him 'a complex classic cuisine, conceived with a watchmaker's precision to preserve the subtlety of the flavour of various products and spices'. Roger Vergé, now his neighbour at Mougins outside Cannes, introduced him to the '*Cuisine du Soleil*'.

Jacques Chibois was recommended for his first head chef's job at the Parisian nightclub, *Regine*, by Michel Guérard. The schooling and promoting of promising protégés is an aspect of the unofficial freemasonry which links the star chefs. Their skills and techniques are constantly cross-fertilizing each other, but each chef retains a distinct personality. The kitchen where they practise their art is both a studio and a laboratory. What comes out of it may be influenced by place or by the season, but it is ultimately a reflection of an individual's imaginative and organizational genius.

When Jacques Chibois opens his own restaurant, as he is bound to, it could be in Paris, Nice or Los Angeles. The location would affect the composition of the menu, but not the style of cuisine. That is a roundabout way of arguing that in the refined world of haute cuisine, a master chef's genius is paramount. Neither Jacques Chibois nor his rival Christian Willer at the *Palme d'Or*, a restaurant in the art-deco *Martinez Hotel* come from Provence. Although they may race each other for the pick of the produce at Cannes' Forville market, they are probably carrying out a similar contest over the telephone for prime produce to be delivered overnight from the Paris market of Rungis. *They* have adopted Provence, rather than vice versa.

Cannes' favourite restaurant with those who come from abroad, *La Mère Besson*, has retained its reputation even though Josephine Besson retired about the same time that the *Royal Gray* was launched. Of the *Mère*'s daily specials, the *aïado* – a boned shoulder of lamb served with a purée of garlic, simmered in white wine to which juices from the roast have been added – is the one that has lasted best. It's served

La Palme d'Or

MARTINEZ

73 LA CROISETTE

06400 CANNES

TELEPHONE 93 68 91 91

La Mère Besson

13 RUE DES FRERES PRADIGNAC

06400 CANNES

TELEPHONE 93 38 94 01

with cubes of fried potato which are tossed in butter and dusted with thyme. *Aïoli* (the complete dish of salt cod and vegetables, not just the garlic sauce), sardines and stuffed rabbit continue to titillate the palates of pilgrims in search of authentic Provençal food. It's curious, but not surprising that Cannois view it as a tourist spot and patronize it less than other bistros. Maybe they are not so wrong after all; a carefully chosen midday meal at the *Royal Gray* may cost no more than a night out chez *La Mère*.

Cannes market
FORVILLE
Daily except Monday

Forville is a concrete structure painted pink which doubles as a car park and covered food market. It's behind the port, and early in the morning fishwives trundle their meagre catch to it in awkward barrows. Even the smallest fish are snapped up within minutes. By 9 am on the day I wandered through the market everything had gone except six tiny fishes on one stall; and they disappeared by 9.20. I had arrived at dawn, when the last of the bleary-eyed teeny-boppers were leaving the all-night discos. In the entrance to the market a lady in slacks threw a plucked chicken in the air and shouted 'Yippie!'; I was too timid to ask her why.

There must be more varied produce – fruit and vegetables especially – on sale here than anywhere along the coast. It's not all from the South of France. One stall specializes in the kind of exotic fruit, rambutan, mangosteens and star fruit, plantains and pineapple, that you might expect to find in Bangkok. Another has violet potatoes from the Gard. Another Arbutus, another two or three types of snail. Another sells flavoured oils in pretty bottles – not successfully, as far as I could judge. But the best displays in the market are the Mediterranean vegetables; curly endives opened out to display their yellow hearts; baby dandelions called *coustelines*; bunches of finger-thin leeks, their roots neatly trimmed; wispy cardoons whose stalks are stewed with anchovy, onion, garlic and parsley; artichokes, aubergines and a dozen kinds of mushroom.

Turn the clock back a few months to the middle of summer and the same abundance would have had a hundred different shapes and colours: clementines; apricots; cherries; Cavaillon melons; courgette flowers; little round courgettes; wild asparagus from Cotignac; beans of all kinds, colours and sizes, and the little spring onions known as *cébettes*.

Aux Bons Raviolis *presents its pasta.*

Aux Bons Raviolis
31 RUE MEYNADIER
06400 CANNES
TELEPHONE 93 39 36 63

La Ferme Savoyarde
22 RUE MEYNADIER
06400 CANNES
TELEPHONE 93 39 63 68

Au Roi du Charolais
38 RUE MEYNADIER
06400 CANNES
TELEPHONE 93 39 09 93

Maiffret
31 RUE D'ANTIBES
06400 CANNES
TELEPHONE 93 39 08 29

Bruno
50 RUE D'ANTIBES
06400 CANNES
TELEPHONE 93 39 25 96

And the joy of going into Forville is that it's hands-on shopping: looking, sniffing, prodding, feeling, even tasting, filling the aluminium bowls put out on some stalls and passing them to be weighed. The stallholders have none of the barrow-boy brashness about them; they are not there to offload duff merchandise at 'bargain' prices. The atmosphere is not impersonal, but it's purposeful and unsentimental. Buyers and sellers get on with a routine job of work. Nobody files up and down the rows mindlessly trolley-pushing like in a supermarket.

The Rue Meynadier which leads down into Forville is, in its own way, every bit as exciting. At No. 31, *Aux Bons Raviolis*, the day's pasta production being arranged in the shop window looks like a kind of surrealist Happening. A succession of raviolis, green ones filled with spinach and ricotta, pink ones with crab or lobster, mushroom-brown ones with *daube* and *cèpes*, plain ones, square ones, round ones, interspaced with ribbon pasta and macaroni emerge from the kitchen and are stacked with extreme care into pre-ordained spaces. During the year Patrick Foppiani may devise 50 separate varieties. The same fastidious attention to window-dressing characterizes *La Ferme Savoyarde*, No. 22, a cheese shop where pristine produce is set out in rows in wicker baskets along one wall. Edouard Ceneri, the owner, is passionate about alpine cheeses, and tends to be scornful of the Provençal ones. Georges Brugère, a master butcher at No. 38 sells *porquetta à la nicoise*, a roasted sucking pig, stuffed with its liver, lungs and kidneys, flavoured with sage, thyme and savory. Between these genuine gems are reliable bakeries, charcuteries, cutlery shops, creameries and grocers' stores.

In comparison, the Rue d'Antibes, the main shopping street seems dull, though it has two luxurious rival confiseries *Maiffret* and *Bruno*. It would be invidious to puff one of these at the expense of the other, but for 20 francs, I bought ten fruit jellies from *Bruno* weighing all of 100 grams. They were, in fact, moulded fruit cheeses, the kind of sweetmeat Victorian parsons' wives enjoyed making. The red fruit ones tasted little different from rubber jam, but a pear one which melted in the mouth was an agreeable surprise. *Bruno* also candies its own clementines, and its bitter chocolates filled with honey and almond praline have the kind of class to appeal to the most pampered *poule de luxe*.

The road from Cannes to Grasse passes through Mougins. This hilltop village is dominated by the *Moulin de Mougins*, Roger Vergé's restaurant. Here he has created an industry based on its brand image. Wines, Provençal herbs, mustards, jams and flavoured vinegars bearing his endorsement are distributed worldwide. Boutiques at the *Moulin* and his second restaurant in Mougins, *l'Amandier* market every conceivable item related to the Art of the Table. He is involved with galas, charity banquets, cookery schools and a Disneyworld restaurant.

On the principle that the best place to locate a restaurant is next door to a successful restaurant, a ring of satellites has appeared. *La Ferme de Mougins, Le Relais de Mougins,* the *Mas Candille* and *Le Bistrot à Mougins* (which, to give it credit, serves a meal for what it would cost to shake hands with Monsieur Vergé), all fly the *Mougins* flag of convenience. Why should Mougins especially attract more than its share of 'fine dining'? Because it can draw not only on the wealth of Cannes, but equally upon the many thousands of rich who have retired to Grasse.

During the Riviera's halcyon period between the wars, Grasse and its surrounding hills had attracted poets, artists and the English. Many of the latter lived in 'quaint' villas, gossiped about their devoted peasant servants and cultivated their gardens. Lady Fortescue, for instance, who wrote a bestseller called *Perfumes from Provence*, delighted in the 'naughty little ways of vegetables'. She was especially impressed by her odd-job man's way with peas and beans: 'He took each bean separately, wrapped it tenderly inside a ball of manure, and deposited it gently in a hole in the ground. Death to a fastidious English seed, but here in Provence, they seem to like it!'

The English influence went out with the tide of lost Empire, leaving little or no trace, except for an odd street name. But the moneyed-classes have remained. I was seeking out Grasse not to sample its perfumes, for which it is the world's capital, nor even to extract the secret formula for Chanel No. 5, from which one Nouvelle Cuisine chef made a sorbet, nor to see the crystallized fruits and flowers being made at the nearby Gorges du Loup, but to search for a stuffed cabbage.

I have to admit in advance that I failed. This may have been for a variety of reasons. The original, old town is compact like many Provençal villages and has its

Moulin de Mougins
QUARTIER NOTRE DAME DE VIE
424 CHEMIN DU MOULIN
06250 MOUGINS
TELEPHONE 93 75 78 24

L'Amandier de Mougins
PLACE DU CDT-LAMY
06250 MOUGINS
TELEPHONE 93 90 00 91

Also in Mougins:

La Ferme de Mougins
10 AVENUE ST-BASIL
TELEPHONE 93 90 03 74

Le Relais de Mougins
PLACE DE LA MAIRIE
TELEPHONE 93 90 03 47

Mas Candille
BOULEVARD REBUFFEL
TELEPHONE 93 90 00 85

Le Bistrot de Mougins
PLACE DU VILLAGE
TELEPHONE 93 75 78 34

share of bistros, bars, cafés and restaurants. But Grasse has become a sprawling township with its own suburbs, clinging to the contours of the foothills on which they stand. Exploring away from the centre takes time. Also, the self-styled King of Stuffed Cabbage, Patrick Boscq who once won a prize from the *Académie de Cuisine* for wrapping a partridge in cabbage leaves (or it might have been stuffing a partridge with a cabbage, I can't remember which) had shut up shop for the day.

Apart from *Maître Boscq*, none of the central restaurants were advertising *sou-fassum*, but I had a tip that *La Serre* in St Jacques-de-Grasse was the place to go. Following the instructions from my source, I caught a bus to a garage on the Draguignan road and was promptly lost. I would have stayed that way, but asked the way from a blind man who wanted me to help him down a stretch of road where there was no pavement. He had lived in Grasse all his life and had known *La Serre* when it opened. He had even peeled vegetables there over a drink with the owner when he had been younger and still had his sight. He gave the perfect directions.

Maître Boscq
13 RUE DE LA FONTETTE
06130 GRASSE
TELEPHONE 93 36 45 76

La Serre
20 AVENUE FELIX-RAYBAUD
06130 ST JACQUES-DE-GRASSE
TELEPHONE 93 70 80 89

From the outside, *La Serre* looked like the ideal Provençal bistro. The patronne who greeted me was the epitome of the jolly hostess – short and rounded. She was from Périgord on the other side of France, and had bought the restaurant just three weeks before. Unfortunately, the *sou-fassum* was even more of a mystery to her than it was to me. She had never heard of it. Instead, she served me a delicious warm salad with duck skins and good oil, a tripe sausage with chips – old-fashioned ones cut quite thick but crisp on the outside – and a bottle of *Château d'Estandon*, a red Côtes de Provence. Because she saw that I was on foot and that there would be no taxis available to return to the centre of Grasse, she persuaded her husband to drop the waiting and run me back into town.

My quest continued, and later in the day, I learnt that *sou-fassum* is prepared by blanching a whole cabbage in boiling water, pulling off the outer leaves and opening out the rest. The heart is removed and chopped up with a pork, veal, rice, egg and garlic stuffing, which is then enveloped in the leaves. The re-formed cabbage is placed in a special net called a *fassumié* and lowered into a simmering stock-pot to cook.

This tit-bit of information came from a unique museum in Villeneuve-Loubet. I took the train there. The local railway station, just outside Cagnes-sur-Mer, with

Master Butcher in Rue Meynadier, the best food street in Cannes.

Musée de l'Art Culinaire
06270 VILLENEUVE-LOUBET
(village)
TELEPHONE 93 73 93 79

the sea on one side and a string of superstores on the other, creates an altogether false impression of what to expect. The village itself, six kilometres away from the station, is sleepy and unspoilt. Here in 1846, in the local blacksmith's home, Auguste Escoffier was born.

Escoffier is the Master who is revered with almost religious awe by the world's chefs, s much for raising their social status as for writing their 'Bible', *Le Guide Culinaire*. Pierette, the Museum of Culinary Arts' assistant curator pointed out a man in the small library who was reading a copy with the fervour of a mullah. 'He's a chef,' she said. 'He told me that he wanted to touch a copy of the first edition.' The Museum, which is also the headquarters of the Fondation Escoffier, dedicated to perpetuating the cause of French gastronomy, is less a historical collection of cookery bric-à-brac than a celebration of Escoffier's life and influence.

As a boy, Auguste had ambitions to be a poet and a sculptor, but his father insisted that he was going to become a cook. So at the age of 13 he was sent to Nice to work for his uncle François. It was 1859, the year before the city, hitherto part of Italy, became part of France. He stayed in Nice throughout his four-year apprenticeship and then found a summer job at a restaurant there, the *Frères Provençaux*.

Escoffier left for Paris before his twentieth birthday and was employed at the *Petit Moulin Rouge*, which by his own account sounded like a high-class knocking shop. It had four public rooms and over 20 small ones for discreet entertaining. Privileged clients, such as The Prince of Wales, Abd-El-Kader and Gambetta went in and out through a private entrance and were known to gorge on dinners of a dozen courses or more.

When he was still only 30, Escoffier bought himself a grocery in Cannes, to which he added a restaurant during the winter season. The small fishing port was just becoming a fashionable resort to rival Nice, but Escoffier later sold up and headed back to Paris, and then to Monte Carlo, where his collaboration with the world-famous hotelier César Ritz began. Ritz was appointed manager of the Savoy Hotel in London and he invited Escoffier to oversee the kitchens there. When the novelist Emile Zola, who had grown up in Provence, visited the Savoy, he spent long hours discussing the merits of Provençal food: 'One would have believed,'

Escoffier recalled in his memoires, 'that he was sitting at table in front of a mutton stew accompanied by a cabbage stuffed in the manner of Grasse.'

Given Escoffier's own obvious sympathy for the dishes of his native Provence it is ironic that the creation for which he is most remembered, invented during his London period, was the *Pêche Melba*, a peach sitting on vanilla ice cream and coated in raspberry sauce. There is a full-length profile of Dame Nellie Melba on a wall of the museum in Villeneuve-Loubet. The rounded haunches of the diva are a hint, no more, at what was going on in Escoffier's mind when he was devising his *chef d'oeuvre*.

At Villeneuve-Loubet, the main downstairs room is described as a 'Provençal kitchen'. On a shelf above the fireplace where Escoffier's mother would have simmered her *daubes* is a row of copper moulds and pots which no working-class Provençal family would have used or needed. In another corner are the stiletto-like *attelets*, the silver skewers used as part of the ornamental centrepieces of grand buffets. The earthenware crocks for the salted meat or honey, the *tians* and the *daubes*, where are they? The odd plate, the odd dish are tucked away in a side-room.

Upstairs is a collection of 15,000 menus taken from transatlantic liners, palaces and Grand Hotels the world over. With an almost painful monotony they repeat the same formula: caviar, consommé, fish, a string of meat, poultry and game courses, salad, vegetables and a dessert. Escoffier certainly devoted his career to the greater glory of French cuisine, but he may have abandoned his Provençal origins in the process.

Of all the exhibits at Villeneuve-Loubet, the one which caught my eye was a small, naïve painting near the entrance. A man looking like Escoffier is lying on his death bed in a delirious trance. Lobsters, geese and chickens are flying round his head. It's a humorous reminder of the fate awaiting those who live only for food.

11

SALT ROAD THROUGH THE MOUNTAINS

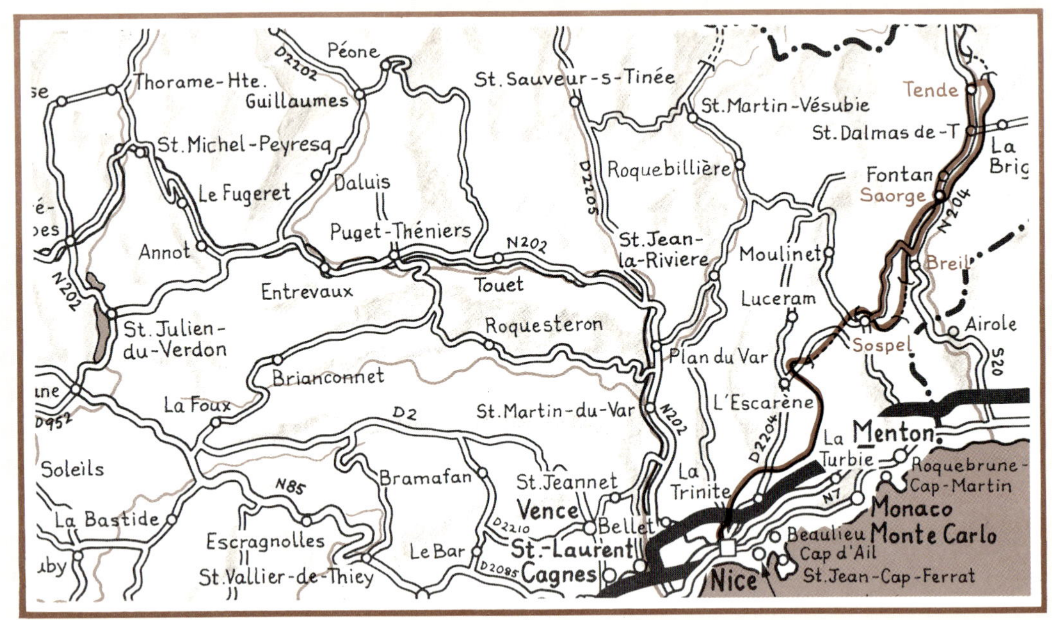

Nice – Tende – Saorge – Breil – Sospel

When Escoffier started his apprenticeship in the County of Nice, he was entering a foreign country, the moment he crossed the River Var. The city-state belonged to the House of Savoy which had held the city and the hinterland behind it for close on 500 years. Regardless of its allegiance, it was still a Provençal centre in spirit and when a referendum was held to confirm the transfer to France in 1860, the inhabitants voted overwhelmingly for France.

Nice had already been 'discovered' by the itinerant English gentry by this time: the ex-patriate colony which had put down roots there had financed the building of a coastal road which became known as the Promenade des Anglais. Among the first to set the fashion for bathing in the Mediterranean was Tobias Smollett, author and one time ship's doctor.

To judge by all the recipes ending *à la niçoise* one might suspect that Nice had a unique cookery style. It does, and the urbane mayor, Jacques Medecin, has written a book to prove it. But the term itself is something of a red herring, because it is often applied to dishes splashed with a tomato, onion and garlic sauce. The food is more interesting than that, because it reflects the overlapping and meeting of two related but distinct cultures: Mediterranean French and Piedmontese Italian. According to M. Medecin it echoes the Niçois identity: 'Not French: we did not like them here. And not Italian, because the Ligurians were cruel.'

When Niçois peasants harvest the local Cailletier olives, little jet beads, they always start by going to the trees at the top of the hill or terrace and work their way back down. It's the most economical way of coping with the back-breaking work. Following their logic, I decided to explore the County of Nice, which stretches up into the Alps, from the top – its border with Italy at Tende – to the bottom. I caught the train to Tende late on a Sunday afternoon, when it was packed with Piedmontese who had been visiting husbands or family working on the Côte d'Azur. It was as much a sentimental as a practical journey for me, because the Nice – Cuneo route is one of the most spectacular railway lines in the world, and there is talk of it being closed to passengers.

The first few miles, escaping from suburbs only to confront scarred quarries, gives little hint of what is in store. But from the moment you glimpse Peillon, a village perched on a spur like a Buddhist monastery, between a series of tunnels before Escarène the scenery becomes magical. Terraces, some planted with vines, others with olive groves carve giant steps up the rocky slopes. Beyond Breil, when an Italian driver and guard replace the French crew, the track climbs up through the Gorges de Saorge and then the Gorges de Bergue, where the Roya courses through the valley, and mountains rise to 1000, 1500, then 2000 metres on either side.

Stepping from the cocoon of a carriage on to the platform at Tende, with the short dusk almost swallowed by night, two hours after basking in sea and warm sunshine is an eerie experience – more striking than flying from one continent to another. The air is dry. The temperature, dropping by the minute, promises frost. Except for the occasional car hurrying through the main street towards the border, Tende is quiet. Above the village on a crest, a tower topped with a pepper-pot belvedere is lit by arc lamps.

Tende has been shunted to and fro between France and Italy over the centuries. When the County of Nice became French, Italy kept the village so that King Victor Emmanuel could follow his passion for hunting. After the Second World War, it reverted to France. The inhabitants have a sensible, ambivalent attitude to their dual nationality. The war memorial in the main square exalts their courageous sons who died, '*caduti per la patria*', '*tombés pour la patrie*'. The hotel where I stayed spoke both languages interchangeably. In the café, youths spoke French but played Italian records.

José Molinari
RUE DE FRANCE
TENDE
TELEPHONE 93 04 60 89

To obtain a bird's eye view of the village, I followed the *montées*, steep, cobbled lanes and steps uphill towards the tower. They led to a closed gate in a rough stone wall with a sign *Resurrecturis* above it. It opened on to a miniature necropolis. Monuments and sarcophagi lay in shadow, but little red candlelit nightlights glowed on the graves. Like wrapping paper being crumpled, the sounds of the Roya filtered up from the valley. The clock in the belvedere struck seven tuneless pickaxe blows, followed by a church below and seconds later by another further off.

A bakery *José Molinari* was just closing when I got back to the centre of the village, and I bought myself a couple of large slices of the local *tourtes*. They were twin-crusted pies baked in shallow trays. The thin pastry, folded and not much thicker than strudel paste, had gone soft – which was not surprising because it had probably been baked that morning – but their substantial fillings seemed perfectly suited to the remote setting and the chill Alpine air.

One contained Swiss chard, a leaf vegetable with edible stalks, chopped small and mixed with eggs and spinach. Both the leaves and stalks of chard feature in many Provençal recipes, in stuffed aubergines, raviolis, and sometimes even in a sweet tart. An old Niçois recipe *capouns*, uses the leaves as a parcel to wrap a stuffing made with the stalks, sausagemeat, rice and herbs.

The other *tourte*, filled with potato, marrow and pumpkin, was more solid and down-to-earth. Except in isolated spots, rustic pies like these are an endangered species. But 'rustic' is the wrong word to describe them, since they are direct descendants of the *tourte d'espinoches* described in the 600-year-old *Viandier*, the first cookery book to be written in French. It is the work of Philip de Valois' master cook, Taillevent. The recipe begins:

> *Pour faire une tourte, prener perressi, mente, espinoches, letuees, marjolienne, basilique et pilieux* . . .

(To make a *tourte*, take parsley, mint, spinach, lettuce, marjoram, basil and pound them . . .)

Tende is on the Salt Road which linked Nice with Turin. During the Middle Ages, salt had the value of hard currency and formed the basis of a sales tax, the *gabelle*, which was collected by inspectors, or 'gabelle farmers'. When Amadeus VII, Count of Savoy, annexed the County of Nice from Provence in 1388, he insisted on extracting his grain of salt from the newly loyal subjects. And later, when Nice was attached to the Count's province of Piedmont, the salt-tax collectors were charged with building a road which would link Nice with Turin. The task fell naturally to them, because salt was the main commodity of value being moved between the two cities. The Salt Road, or its modern equivalent the N204, follows the meanderings of the Roya across the Italian border and down to the coast.

Early next morning, with a thick crust of frost on the ground, and the daylight

Clamped to a cliff-face, Saorge remains remote and unspoilt.

Sospel's 10th-century bridge spans the River Bévera.

still trapped beneath the ridge of mountains along the Italian border, I started back down this ancient highway and headed for Saorge. The village is off the N204, separated from the outside world by a tunnel. In a car it would take a few seconds to cross. On foot it's a long, oppressive journey: more so when a van hurrying through drove an echoing blast off the walls which made me feel like a spider stuck half way up a French horn.

On the other side of the tunnel, Saorge emerged, clamped to a cliff-face, with the sun's first diagonal rays filtered through wisps of cloud picking out the detail of its rooftops. Saorge is classed as a 'Monumental Village' like Rocamadour in the South-West of France and Gordes in the Vaucluse. But it's so isolated that it could never support the infrastructure of boutiques, potteries, gift shops and cafés which symbolize the annual tourist pilgrimages to those places. Instead, it is a totally unspoilt, rock-solid throwback to the Middle Ages, with no special places of interest worth visiting except for the place itself.

Inside the perimeter of grey stone-walled houses, some seven or eight storeys high, is a tangle of passages where two people can barely walk abreast without slipping into the gutter. They wind upwards in anarchic fashion to the higher reaches of the village, sometimes burrowing under houses, sometimes ending in steps, sometimes veering off from the way they were pointing to exit in the church square. They are grey, cool and shadowy.

The bakery, no more than a cubby-hole in a row of 15th-century tenements, was closed, but a hand-printed sign outside drew attention to 'PICORES DE SAORGE'. I rapped on a glass-fronted door next to the shop. The baker was eating breakfast, and I apologized for disturbing him, explaining my curiosity about his '*Picores*'. He got up and fetched me one from a glass cabinet: it was a large, glazed bun, fashioned like a turban, with eight segments around a decorated axis. It was an old recipe, he told me, which he had discovered in the village's archives when he became the local baker. Was I interested in his bread? Monday was his day off; he would show me his oven.

I expected it to be at the back of his shop, but it turned out to be in another building down the street, in a dingy room which had probably remained unchanged for at least a century. 'I don't own the oven,' the baker told me. 'It's what is known as a *four banal*. It belongs to the community. I have its use in exchange for baking for the village.'

The oven was identical to the one I had seen in Sarrians. It was big enough to roast a lamb whole, which the baker had done for a friend's wedding. He had put it in when he'd finished the day's bread, keeping the fire just ticking over with *petit bois*, small wood.

He was proud of his craft. 'All my bread is organic,' he boasted, showing me sacks of flour with the 'Nature and Progress' symbol. Then, from behind a curtain, he brought out a yellow basin filled with a brown-seething mass. He went on: 'Plenty of bakers say that they're baking organic bread, but they aren't. They buy yeast, which is an artificially produced form of fungus – whereas I work from a basic leaven, which is created entirely by the activity of bacteria.'

He dug his hand into the sticky ferment. The mixture had a strong aroma, similar to old wine vinegar. This was his 'Chef', the biological raising agent of which he added a small amount to all his loaves – but not directly. A piece of it went to form the 'second' leaven, which was the starter of each batch of bread.

Although he loved baking, he was planning to leave Saorge. For years, he complained, he had supplied the only bread made in Saorge and never received any thanks. He and his family were going off to live in a tepee village.

Later that morning I met another kind of what the French like to call 'Marginals'. Coming into Saorge I had noticed a poster advertising a 'Chestnut Feast', and underneath it in large letters the word '*Brousse*'. The baker had told me it was a cheese which some of the farmers produced with their spare milk. I wondered whether it was the same as the *Brousse de Rove* I had tasted at the *Clos de la Violette*.

After leaving him and taking two or three wrong turnings, I found a poorly-lit grocery several steps below street level. The lady behind the counter had a dozen manufactured cheeses for sale. No, she did not have any Brousse, but one of her customers – a middle-aged woman in a track-suit and rubber boots – did.

The woman in wellingtons and I quit the shop together and zig-zagged down some alleys until we reached the cellar where she kept her personal stock of preserves.

She had a row of buff spheroid *tommes*, pressed mountain cheeses, the size of cannon balls. Often they are prepared from sheep or goat's milk, but she preferred cow's. She cut me a slice to taste: the yellow paste was pitted with bubbles, a bit like gruyère, but the taste was unique. It was mature but not overpowering, slightly rancid at the edge but clean-tasting and grassy in the centre.

Did she sell this wonder to the outside world? 'You know what it's like,' she said. 'People around these parts want supermarket products. They always imagine that if it comes from somewhere else it must be better!'

On rows of slatted wooden racks were her winter stores of vegetables in sterilized bottles: tomatoes and tomato purée, green beans and the white haricot beans nicknamed 'cocos' in Provence, and olives in abundance. To one side was a pair of yellow, plastic dustbins covered with immaculate cloths. In these she stored '*Le Broux*'. Here, she insisted upon the distinction. '*La Brousse*' was the fresh cottage cheese, but '*Le Broux*', she pronounced it the same way, was many months old. She explained that *Le Broux*, was what the shepherds took with them to eat in their mountain cabins. At night, when it grew cold, they grilled a crust of bread over the embers and spread a thin layer of the cheese over it and maybe toasted it gently once more like a Welsh rarebit, before tucking in. It warmed their insides.

After sniffing it, I could understand why this was a cheese for taking to a lonely hillside. It was strong enough to frighten off wolves. Once swallowed it induced a sensation akin to an attack of acid indigestion. Rotten cheese might be one way of describing it, but perhaps that's the sort of thing that overcivilized beings who turn up their noses at over-ripe camembert might say. It becomes warming and almost pleasant after a while.

It had the kind of robust taste, I suggested, which would need a good *pain de campagne* to do it justice. She picked up the inference. Yes, she admitted, the baker baked '*bon pain*', but she was not too impressed by the man. Most people in Saorge were peasants, she explained. They wanted to buy bread at six in the morning, but he refused to sell it before eight.

In the tiny community, the two positions had obviously grown entrenched. On the one hand, the largely elderly population expected the service they felt it was a

Delicate cheeses in harsh sunlight at Sospel.

baker's historical duty to provide. Meanwhile, he grew frustrated that he received no credit, despite devoting such care to his work.

Madame qualified her criticism by admitting that the members of her own family were not peasants, but good farming stock. They always bought enough bread for several days, and they never ate it fresh because it was indigestible. The baker's loaves kept for a week, no problem, but – I must understand – her loyalties were with the villagers.

I bought a jar of *Le Broux* scraped from the deeper recesses of one of the bins, and set off for Breil, the next village down the Salt Road. A small food fair was in progress on the main road, opposite an emerald lake fed by the Roya. It had stalls selling cheeses, honey, chestnuts, and olives from the terraced slopes around the commune. Yet, sadly, the only queue I saw had formed to buy overpriced, garish boiled sweets.

Close to the parish church, Sancta-Maria-in-Albis, is an unpretentious inn, *Chez Anna*, which prepares another of the County of Nice's edible relics. *Boursottos*, little purses, are crunchy pasties stuffed with rice, leeks, spinach, anchovy and parmesan. Both the name and the ingredients are reminders that Italy is close by. Between Breil and the border eight kilometres away lies a hamlet called Libre (Freedom). It came into being because Italian convicts, escaping from a jail close to the frontier, knew that they had reached France and safety once they had arrived.

The French N204 becomes the Italian S20 at Libre. To return to Nice along that route, I would have had to cross into Italy, work my way down to Ventimiglia and catch a train. Instead, I chose to hitch to Sospel through the Col de Brouis, a switchback pass linking the Roya and Bévera valleys. Almost the first vehicle to pass stopped for me. The driver was a Portuguese immigrant who sucked aniseed balls loudly throughout the journey. He offered to drive me as far as Nice, but I thanked him and explained that I wanted to spend an hour or so in Sospel.

Although a picture-postcard village, with a 10th-century bridge crossing the river Bévera, Sospel lacks the dramatic impact of villages in the upper Roya. It's more of a base-camp for those about to explore the Mercantour National Park which stretches in a wide band across Provence's north-east border with Italy.

In the back of my mind I had a disjointed memory that Sospel was noted for a kind of raisin-studded brioche flavoured with aniseed, known as *crechente*. But nobody I asked – including two girls working in the Mairie, Town Hall, a grocer and a lady marching down the promenade beside the river with four baguettes under her arm – knew anything about it.

What the two employees at the Mairie told me was that *bausias*, 'Little lies', were the 'Specialité de la ville'. Not knowing whether I was on a wild goose chase, I followed their lead and tracked down 'little lies' in a patisserie run by Thiérry Lallavena. He described himself as a silly old bugger from before the war (the translation of his words is approximate but conveys the meaning) and then he gave me his own recipe.

Bausias are little cakes handed round at weddings and christenings, but the patisserie made them all year, because there was a demand. He gave me his own recipe which I took down verbatim: '500 grams flour, 150 grams softened butter, 150 grams sugar, a coffee spoon of salt, a few drops of orange flour water and three eggs. Separate the eggs and whisk the egg white to a snow. Cream the butter, sugar, salt, half a sachet of baking powder, orange flower water and yolks. Combine them with the flour and fold in the whites. Rest the paste, roll it out as finely as you can and cut it into strips two or three centimetres wide. Out of these form knots or little shells, drop them in the deep fryer and when they are done, sprinkle them with icing sugar.'

The formula works, up to a point, but the cunning old fox knew that he was not giving away the real secret: years of experience, handling the paste, living with it, getting its feel, so that preparing it becomes second nature.

Did *he* know anything about the *crechente* I was searching for? All he could think of were *grisses*, hoop-shaped buns made like the *pognes* in the Vaucluse, but flavoured with orange and aniseed. Perhaps the source which suggested *crechentes* as a Sospel speciality got it wrong. Maybe is was just '*bausias*' – little lies.

As I approached the ticket office, the strains of a Mozart flute concerto echoed along the empty platform. I listened until it stopped, before venturing into the hall to buy my ticket and thank the station master for his recital. He wasn't very skilled,

The road that leads from Nice to the mountains.

Nice's picturesque old quarter.

Espuno
35 RUE DROITE
06000 NICE
TELEPHONE 93 80 50 67

Boulangerie de la Cathédrale
8 RUE MASCOINAT
06000 NICE

Nissa Socca
5 RUE STE-REPARATE
06000 NICE
TELEPHONE 93 80 18 35

René Socca
2 RUE MIRALHETTI
06000 NICE
TELEPHONE 93 62 37 81

he demurred, but he enjoyed playing. Judging by the number of trains which stop in Sospel, he would have had plenty of time to practise. Politely, he told me that the next train into Nice was not for an hour, so he was locking the station and going for a pastis – which he did.

Returning to a modern city after my excursion to the County of Nice's inner recesses left me wondering how such different life-styles could co-exist so close to each other without touching. But of course, they do affect each other. The Saorgeois want to buy the heavily packaged supermarket produce. Affluent Niçois search out the food shops and restaurants which remind them of their disappearing heritage.

To buy bread, for instance, they go to *André Espuno* whose *fougasses* and *fougassettes* flavoured with orange-flower water, olive or aniseed contrast with the factory-style baguettes sold by most of the city's bakeries. He is not the only one to bake with a wood-fired oven. In Nice's old quarter, the *Boulangerie de la Cathédrale* does as much. It also produces the flat round *panbagnats*, large baps filled with salade niçoise, which are meals in themselves.

During the day, Niçois of all classes thrive on street food. The best and worst of the many savoury morsels is *pissaladière*, an onion tart studded with black olives. Nearly all the boulangeries sell it, but it can be an awful let-down, even when it's fresh. The trick is to slice the onions, and stew them very slowly until they reduce to a brown syrupy marmalade. The base should be thin and very crisp. The best I ever tasted, years ago, was made with puff pastry, not a yeast dough at all.

More typical still is *socca*, a crusty and quite peppery pancake made from chickpea flour, baked on a griddle. Bars and bistros keep a constant stream of *socca* cooking throughout the day, but it's the *Nissa-Socca* in the Rue Ste-Réparate or *René Socca* in the Rue Miraletti, where the demand is most constant and the supply, therefore, freshest.

Any ice-cream lover should make a bee-line to *Fenocchio*. You can sit outside in the sunshine sipping fruit juices while you eat, or carry away cornets filled with mandarin or grapefruit sorbets, or ice-creams flavoured with honey and pine kernel or even nougat.

Fenocchio is in the Place Rossetti opposite the Church of Ste-Réparate. The church is the hub of Old Nice, a tangle of streets so awkward to negotiate that taxi drivers refuse to enter it. Set behind the Cours Saleya, a market more charming visually than Forville, though less well stocked, it is a quarter where Niçois go to forget they belong to a city. The cafés, bars and restaurants here cost less than those on the main boulevards, and both the quality of food and the friendliness of service are in a different class.

At the *Taverne du Château*, packed every night, waiters in green pullovers process orders at the double. Order a bottle of Bandol, *Château La Rocque*: two minutes later it's at the table, opened and ready to drink. Salade niçoise? A fresh bowl is there before you can pour the wine into the glass. *Daube de boeuf*? Large chunks of beef are piled on to a vast plate in a sauce that smells of *cèpes* and is flecked with pieces of carrot and onion.

The all-in-one alternative to hunting for Nice's best-loved foods is to visit *Barale*, where Hélène Barale has served a choiceless *table d'hôte* and the same Pierrefeu wine for longer than most Niçois can remember. Of course, it's for the tourists, but even Jacques Medecin goes there occasionally. The menu includes *socca*, salade niçoise, *daube* and ravioli and for dessert there is a sweet tart made with '*blettes*' (Swiss chard) and raisins.

There are three dining-rooms at *Barale*, all crammed with brasses, copper, baskets, bottles, jars, cart-horse yokes and enough bric-à-brac to start an antique shop. In one room is a Trèfle, the vintage car which Hélène's mother drove before the Second World War, when the premises were a general store. It's the kind of place where it pays to drink deep, because when the eating ends it may be time to start singing '*Nica la bella*'.

Fenocchio
2 PLACE ROSSETTI
06000 NICE

La Taverne du Château
42 RUE DROITE
06000 NICE
TELEPHONE 93 62 37 73

Barale
39 RUE BEAUMONT
06000 NICE
TELEPHONE 93 89 17 94

12

THE PINE-CONE TRAIN

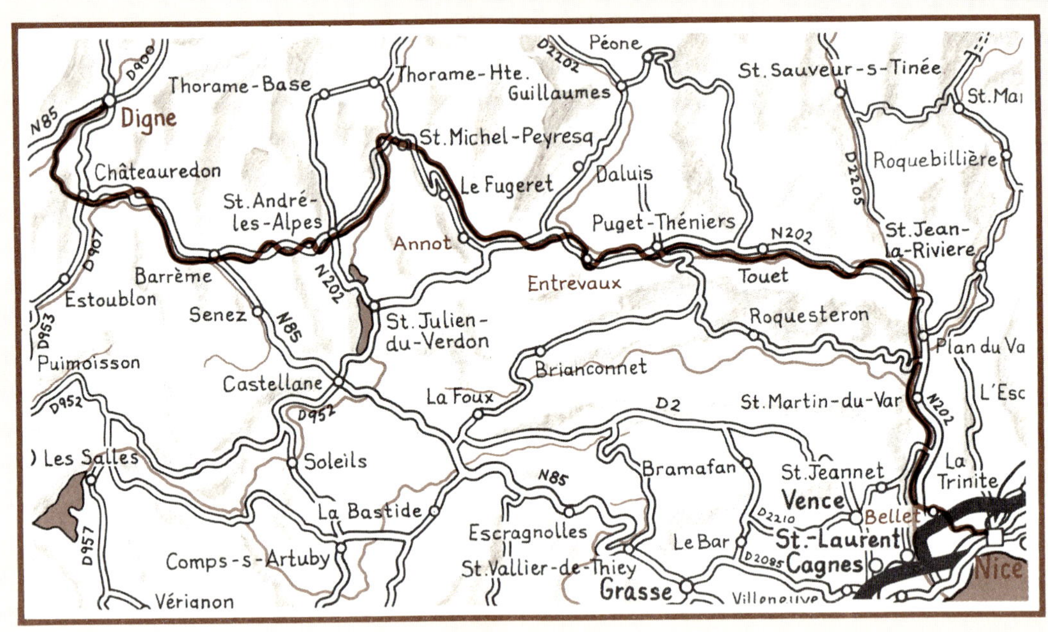

Nice – Bellet – Entrevaux – Annot – Digne

I decided to make my exit along the old *Chemin de Fer de la Provence* from Nice to Digne. It's a narrow-gauge railway which starts at sea-level and climbs 1000 metres into the lower reaches of the Alps. It is run by a privately owned company rather than the national railway, and the guards, ticket collectors and drivers have the same loose-necked manner that you might expect on a country bus service.

Although the steam engine which pulled a couple of toy carriages has now been replaced by a glorified tram, the journey has lost none of its charm. It rattles out of the antiquated station at the top of Avenue Malaussena and into Nice, halting the traffic as it crosses busy streets. Beyond, it stops to order for whoever sticks out an arm from beside the track.

Still within the commune of Nice, it brushes the miniature wine-growing region of Bellet. Like the vineyards around Cassis, the vines here are threatened by encroaching urban development. But the best parcels of cultivated land are safely situated high above the river Var, on slopes so steep in places that the rotivators used for clearing the strips between the rows have to be pulled by a winch.

The site has a unique microclimate. During the day the sea-breezes gust through the valley; by night currents of cold alpine air flow down it. The constant aeration of the plants keeps them free of disease and allows the grapes to ripen completely before harvest. Rosés and red wines are more abundant, but the most sought after are the dry whites. These are made from a grape variety, Rolle, which may perhaps be a descendant of the original vinestocks planted by the Phocian Greek colonists. Rolle is found nowhere else in France. It gives a fruity, moderately alcoholic wine with plenty of finesse.

Bellet's reputation goes back 300 years. Louis XIV's Maréchal Catinet wrote to the Governor of Nice: 'You ask me what I think of the Bellet you sent me. Without being polite, I can assure you that it was found to be admirable and impressed us more than all the wines of France which we had here, though they were good and well-chosen.'

There are only four estates in Bellet of which *Château Crémat* is the one which appears on the wine lists of the grand restaurants between Monte Carlo and Cannes.

The name has a Latin origin (*cremare*, to burn) and the property was once the site of a warning beacon. The château itself, owned by Charles Bagnis, is only a century old, a mock-medieval fortress, built on a series of underground galleries (now the vineyard cellars) quarried by the Romans for building materials.

Once past Bellet, the railway line hugs the left bank of the Var. Stretched out on either side of it are smallholdings, some of them not so small, where many of the flowers, tiny vegetables and salads which adorn the markets between Cannes and Monte Carlo are grown. Despite the warm autumn sunshine, most were protected by cloches or by polythene tunnels as I passed. Hidden from view were the delicate plants destined to be sold as *plançons* or *mesclun*, the beans and tomatoes for a salade niçoise, the aubergines and courgettes for *ratatouille*.

At Plan du Var, the River Var is joined by its main tributary, the Vésubie, and the Mediterranean hinterland comes to an abrupt halt. River, railroad and the main N202 suddenly dive into the Défilé du Chaudan, a narrow funnel of a gorge where the waters rubbing the limestone bed turn a pale eau-de-nil. Inside the little carriage, the change is almost palpable; heads turn to pick out details in the scenery; strangers begin conversations; the guard chats with the regulars.

The upper Var valley from the village of La Tinée is a broad, lush strap of land with neat peach and pear orchards, flanked by the heavily wooded mountain slopes. I got off in Entrevaux. It's a perfectly intact fortified village dominated by a ruined castle perched on a crag. It was built by Louis XIV's military engineer, Maréchal Vauban, of whom it was said that no fort to which he laid siege ever held out, and no castle for which he had prepared the defences was taken.

Entrevaux's citadel must have appealed to his imagination. To reach it an attacking force would have had to scale a series of zig-zagging cobblestone ramps, protected by 20 bastioned gates under the defenders' fire. Just to climb them now is an achievement, but having done so, there are no turnstiles to pass through, no guided tours, just a series of wonderful views along the Var through the sockets of ruined windows.

One hundred and fifty metres below, the weathered terracotta rooftops of the village, framed by the river swinging around it in a hairpin bend, form a perfect exclamation point tapering down to the dot of the old cathedral tower. Even without its fort, the village would have been able to keep out marauding bands. The Var provides a natural protective moat spanned by a drawbridge with its own gatehouse.

In the square, a rather grand word for an irregularly shaped space, is a charcuterie, *Lovera*, specializing in mountain hams, sausages and *secca*, air dried beef similar to the Italian *bresaola*. At the café next door, the barman – a giant with an ill-fitting wig – was planning a boar-hunt with his customers. Nailed to a door in an alley a sign advertised *Charbon de Bois*, charcoal. The whole feel of the village seemed tuned in to the surrounding hills.

What caught my eye was a printed poster in a window announcing: LES JOURNEES MY COLOGIQUES D'ENTREVAUX – 1988. It was an advertisement for a mushroom congress which had taken place the previous weekend. Pencilled in as the theme for the conference was the provocative title: 'Edible Mushrooms, DANGER beware!!'

Naturally, I wanted to discover more. The *Syndicat d'Initiative* could not help. It did not have any information on the annual mushroom gathering, except that there had been an exhibition at the headquarters of the village's fire brigade. I should go and visit Dr Lucien Giacomono who organized the event.

His house was up a back-road across the Var, on the way into the hills. The house-keeper who answered the door thought that I had come as a patient and told me that the doctor was unavailable. But when I explained that I was not so much interested in his medical services as his mushrooms, she changed her tune. It was true that he was not at home, but she would contact him at the hospital. Would I like to sit down in the surgery waiting-room?

The doctor arrived within 15 minutes, a balding, bearded man in early middle age. If he had missed a stitch sewing up a patient in order to see me so promptly, he did not show it. Mushrooms were his hobby and his passion. If I looked back along the Var valley, he said, I would notice that on one side mostly broad-leaf trees grew, especially varieties of oak. On the other was pine forest. Well, each habitat had its own characteristic kinds of wild mushrooms. The conifers attracted the species such as *lactarius deliciosus*, but *cèpes* and *chanterelles* grew in deciduous woods.

Lovera
by
PORTE NATIONALE
ENTREVAUX

Entrevaux, where locals hunt for wild boar and wild mushrooms.

Preparing for the feast at Annot's Buffet de la Gare.

Entrevaux's annual conference had both a popular and a serious side, the doctor explained. It organized mushroom gathering expeditions for the public which helped those with a casual interest to identify edible and inedible varieties. The scientific seminars sought to extend the knowledge about mushrooms: 'small chemical factories into which Man has only entered very timidly', he called them.

'It could be,' Doctor Giacomono intimated, 'that 20 years from now, mushrooms will no longer be edible.'

The real threat, he explained, was not that we would accidentally poison ourselves by eating a deadly Avenging Angel or Death Cap amanite, but that the field and wood mushrooms which have always been picked by country people were potentially toxic.

At the most basic level, mycologists cannot agree on a catalogue of which wild fungus are edible and which may be poisonous. Local by-laws in Provence permit the sale in markets of species which have on occasion been proven to be fatal. The False Morel has killed, but it may legally be sold in Avignon. *Clavaria formosa*, a spindly fungus, can be bought in Nice, but it can make those who eat it very ill. The variety of *boletus*, known as the *pissacan* in Provence provokes surprise purges. Even the giant parasol mushroom, sold by the crate in Paris's central market, Rungis, caused a series of poisoning outbreaks during the 1970s, whereas they had been considered 'safe' from time immemorial.

To me the implication that eating any wild mushroom is a kind of gourmet's Russian roulette added to, rather than diminished from, the charm. There is no way that any legislation can ever prevent individuals from exercising their freedom of choice and going out with a basket to collect what the poet Corneille described as 'Nature's rare excrement'.

Unfortunately, the natural risk is minor compared to the effects of man-made pollution. Herbicides, pesticides, lead from petrol fumes and other mineral pollutants are starting to turn hitherto safe mushrooms toxic. It's not too reassuring either to know that some edible mushrooms can contain mutagenes capable of modifying human cells. In passing, Dr Giacomono mentioned that his next congress was going to discuss the curative properties of fungus. Which I wondered, did they do first:

kill or cure? By coincidence, when I caught the train, I glimpsed a sign planted close to the line saying: 'Do not pick mushrooms'. Whether this was an injunction aimed at the Italians who regularly cross the border to gather what they can of the mushroom harvest, or a friendly health warning, I could not be sure.

The *Chemin de Fer de la Provence*'s emblem is a pine cone and the train is referred to affectionately as the *train des pignes*. Beyond Entrevaux, when the Var swerves north and the line heads due west and up through the pine woods, the reason becomes clear.

Annot, the next stop, is like a scaled-up model railway station. It has a water tower, relic of the pre-War steam era, signals and sidings for shunting matchbox trucks. Within view of the platform an elegant viaduct spans a rift valley with the mountain village framed by its arches.

Buffet de la Gare
ANNOT

But its soul is the *Buffet de la Gare*. The moment the *autorail* creaked to a halt on the platform, guard and driver were off for an impromptu coffee at the bar. The passengers who knew the form trooped after them. Two old ladies collected huge chunks of homemade brioche wrapped in foil from the counter and exited munching happily. A coquette blonde with short legs precariously tucked into tight jeans was laying up tables for lunch. I asked her to reserve me one.

Annot itself had a kind of toy-town feel to it, though perhaps my judgement was influenced by the impression which the station had made on me. It was reinforced when I made a telephone call to England from the Post Office: the woman behind the counter only charged me 1F50 a minute. Surely she was undercharging, I said. No, the call had been logged and that was the price. The giant plane trees in the town centre seem too big for the houses. A supermarket on the outskirts looked as though it ought to be a village shop.

At the Chamber of Commerce I inquired whether Annot had any typical drinks or dishes. 'Well,' said the lady behind the counter, 'there are raviolis (she used the Provençal term, *raiolles*), stuffed with marrow and bone marrow served with a walnut and cream sauce.'

Where could I try those, I asked? Unfortunately, she told me, they were only made at Christmas as a seasonal speciality.

'Then, of course,' she went on, 'there are crayfish in the Coulomp.'

Wonderful, I thought. But the hotel which specialized in crayfish was closed until the next season.

'And in winter, the local wine is mulled with cinnamon, but it is not yet winter, Monsieur, is it?'

At Easter, she continued, they roasted a young goat, and Monsieur Fenouil made *catchetti* – which I assumed to be a strong cheese. But Monsieur was away. What I might do, she recommended, was go to the bar next to the butcher Rigau and see if the man who sold chestnut honey was there; he often stopped by for an aperitif about midday. When she began describing the baby *cèpes* eaten raw in salads, I could bear it no more and disappeared ostensibly to find the honey man. After flicking through the local paper and swallowing two bitter coffees, I gave up and headed back to the *Buffet de la Gare*.

I was the first to arrive, but within half an hour, there was not a table to be had. The room filled with a cross-section of the community; painters and decorators, officials, secretaries with their bosses. A pair of builders at the table next to mine, one with a Zapata moustache, the other like a bald Captain Dreyfus discussed real estate. The meal was what the French would have called *la popote*, family cooking in the best possible sense.

A bottle of the patron's wine with its own '*Buffet de la Gare*' label materialized on the table. It turned out to be a good Côtes du Rhône which, he later told me, he bought directly from the grower every year. While I was filling my glass the blonde, now with a frilly apron over her jeans, served me a plate of charcuterie: pâté with mushrooms in it; fresh *saucisson sec* and garlic sausage; plenty of tiny ripe olives, whose flesh fell away from the stones; tomatoes and a diced beetroot salad.

About three glasses into the Côtes du Rhône, as I was studying the faded black and white picture postcards of the *Chemin de Fer de la Provence*'s early days, stuck on a board by the bar, the main dish arrived: stewed leg and shoulder of rabbit with a sauce of puréed marrow, flavoured with rosemary; two slices of polenta, and a pile of green beans.

To finish there was a lemon meringue pie. Obviously, the patronne, Madame

Among the pines near Annot, the viaduct spans the valley.

Domeneck loved baking. The pie had a fine biscuity crust; a tart but melting filling, topped with fluffy meringue. The bill came to less than 100 francs. I felt at peace with the world – not because the cooking was so special, but because it matched the setting and surroundings like a piece in a simple jigsaw puzzle.

As I boarded the 14.19 Pine-cone Train, it started to rain. Between Annot and St André-les-Alpes, clouds tumbled down the slopes into the valleys washing the bare limestone and painting out the landscape. At Chabrières, where the line follows the old Route Napoléon (N85), a rockfall had blocked the track. It took an hour to clear and it was dark before we reached Digne.

The town is Provence's lavender capital. Cultivating the plant as a cash crop only started this century, but it has always grown wild in the uplands of the Var and Vaucluse. Mountain lavender has a feathery leaf which smells aromatic and herby rather than sweet, and its flowers are a deep and intense blue. Most of it is distilled for scent, but it has found its way on to menus in the form of sorbets and ice creams. A little is added to the *Herbes de Provence* mixture which is sold in earthenware jars. The harvest lasts from July to September. I was there in December, and the only strips of lavender bushes I ever saw near Digne looked just like columns of grey-green hedgehogs.

Hôtel du Grand Paris
0400 DIGNE-LES-BAINS
TELEPHONE 92 31 11 15

I booked in at the *Hôtel du Grand Paris*, hoping that Frédéric Mistral's comment that 'Dignois gave the impression of eating in a drawer' had been prejudiced by an unlucky experience. I dined in a virtually empty room, and lingered over an oxtail terrine, guinea fowl, Banon cheese and a bottle of Bandol until the head-waiter hinted that he would like to shut up shop.

Technically, my dinner was more accomplished than my midday meal in Annot. The chef Jean-Jacques Ricaud is a *Maître Cuisinier*, one of France's élite. But I had enjoyed the simpler cooking far more, and I could not help thinking that there are now two kinds of Provençal food.

'*La Cuisine du Soleil*', as interpreted by starred restaurants, uses the marvellous Provençal ingredients, but belongs to the mainstream of French gastronomy. I love the sophistication of this cuisine; the vocabulary which describes dishes as 'exquisite' and 'sublime' is often justified. But I think unrefined, locally-grown food, at its best, tastes better. It *belongs* to a place in an instinctive, unassuming way; it doesn't challenge a gourmet to appreciate the Master Chef's skills.

Provence isn't peopled by gastronomes, but those who live there have year-round access to a store-cupboard of matchless natural produce. Few of the millions who go there will cross the threshold of a three-star restaurant, but all can afford a ripe melon, a fresh tomato salad or a dish of herb-scented black olives.

INDEX

Figures in *italics* refer to illustrations